LOCKHEED BLACKBIRD FAMILY

A-12, YF-12, D-21/M-21 & SR-71
PHOTO SCRAPBOOK

Compiled by Tony R. Landis

specialtypress
PUBLISHERS AND WHOLESALERS

Specialty Press
39966 Grand Avenue
North Branch, MN 55056
Phone: 651-277-1400 or 800-895-4585
Fax: 651-277-1203
www.specialtypress.com

Edit by Mike Machat
Layout by Monica Seiberlich

ISBN 978-1-58007-151-2
Item No. SP151

Library of Congress Cataloging-in-Publication Data

Landis, Tony.
  Lockheed Blackbird family photo scrapbook / by Tony R. Landis.
    p. cm.
  ISBN 978-1-58007-151-2
  1. SR-71 Blackbird (Jet reconnaissance plane)—Pictorial works. 2. SR-71 Blackbird (Jet reconnaissance plane)—History. 3. Aerodynamics, Transonic—Research—United States—History—20th century—Sources. I. Title.
  UG1242.R4L35 2010
  623.74'67—dc22
                                          2009032855

Printed in China
10 9 8 7 6 5 4 3

Distributed in the UK and Europe by
Crécy Publishing Ltd
1a Ringway Trading Estate
Shadowmoss Road
Manchester M22 5LH England
Tel: 44 161 499 0024
Fax: 44 161 499 0298
www.crecy.co.uk
enquiries@crecy.co.uk

Front Cover:
Testing the Linear Aerospike engine proved to be as troublesome as the construction of the actual X-33 vehicle. Despite attempts to fix the problems as they arose, many proved to be insurmountable. With funding running out, the decision was made to cancel the LASRE program in November 1999. Cancellation of the entire X-33 demonstrator program followed 13 months later. The Aerospike engine was then returned to Lockheed and the aeroshell was stored. The "canoe" was also stored for a number of years before it was finally cut up and scrapped. (Jim Ross/NASA DFRC)

Title Page:
SR-71A 61-7972 departs Palmdale performing a heavyweight takeoff on one of its final flights. Blackbird test crews made these dramatic heavy-weight takeoffs due to the lack of tanker support at this point in the program. They were, however, highly impressive for the crowds that would inevitably gather outside that desert airport's perimeter fences. (Tom Rosquin)

Back Cover Top:
Surrounded by work stands and myriad types of ground equipment, the first M-21 is checked over by ground crews before its inaugural flight with a D-21 drone mated to the pylon on its upper rear fuselage. (Lockheed Martin)

Back Cover Bottom:
Known in the Blackbird community as "The Big Tail," this modified SR-71 carried aft-facing Electronic Counter Measures (ECM) equipment and a 24-inch Optical Bar Camera. (Lockheed Martin)

Contents

Acknowledgments

A book such as this does not happen overnight. It has been more than two decades since I first began collecting images and photographing Blackbirds. During this time many people have given of their time, and some have become close friends. Those good friends who deserve special mention are Mike Relja, who has forgotten more about Blackbirds than I will ever know; Denny Lombard of Lockheed Martin, a fellow photographer who has always gone above and beyond the call to help out in any way possible; and Dennis Jenkins, my cohort in crime when it comes to these book projects who, in my opinion, is the best aerospace writer in the business.

The many others who have been of invaluable assistance are David Allison, Gerald Balzer, TD Barnes (Roadrunners Internationale), Blair Bozek, Bill Campbell, Tony Chong, Al Cirino, Larry DeCew, Jim Eastham, Don Emmons, Bill "Flaps" Flanagan, Christopher Freeze, Bob Gilliland, Ron Girouard, Jim Goodall, Art Haynes, Leland Haynes, Kevin Helm, Toni Hiley (curator, CIA Museum), Marty Isham, Freida Johnson (AFFTC History Office), Christian Ledet, Mike Lombardi (Boeing Historical Archives), Betty Love, Mike Machat, Jerry McCulley, Jay Miller, Jerry Miller, Doug Nelson, Daryl Niewald, Terry Panopalis, Jeannette Remak, David Robarge (CIA historian), Tom Rosquin, Mick Roth, Tom Tullis, Jim Tuttle, Scott Wilson, James Young (AFFTC History Office), and NASA Dryden Flight Research Center. Special thanks to each and every one of you; this book would not exist without your help.

Tony R. Landis
Tehachapi, California

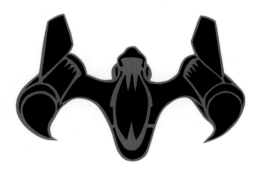

During its brief 20-month assignment to flight-test duties in 1980 and 1981, SR-71A 61-7974 was involved in flying Space Shuttle descent and approach patterns to test NASA's TACAN and S-band communication systems. (NASA)

Introduction

It has been nearly 50 years since construction began on the first of Lockheed's Blackbirds and more than a decade has passed since one last graced the skies, yet these magnificent vehicles continue to fascinate and inspire anyone who comes in contact with one.

The history of the Lockheed Blackbird family has been well documented over the years by authors such as Jay Miller, Dennis R. Jenkins, Paul Crickmore, and Col. Richard Graham, just to name a few. Each year more details about their operations are declassified and we learn even more about those formerly secret missions.

This book does not attempt to give a detailed account of the Blackbird family's history but provides a historical photographic record using recently declassified and rarely seen images from the days when Blackbirds were queens of the sky. Added to that are tidbits and stories that usually don't appear in the larger histories.

From its first flight in April 1962 until that final flight in October 1999, the Blackbird family proved to be remarkable aircraft. From carrying cameras or missiles in its internal bays to carrying the D-21 drone or the Linear Aerospike engine testbed on its back, flying secret missions over denied territory or research missions for NASA, the Blackbirds proved to be versatile and reliable aircraft despite all of the demands of flying at their normal operating environment of Mach 3+ speeds and altitudes in excess of 80,000 feet.

For those of you interested in production numbers, there were fifteen A-12s, three YF-12As, and thirty-two SR-71s built by Lockheed for a grand total of fifty Blackbirds. In a fitting tribute to this remarkable vehicle, the Blackbird family remains the only operational aircraft to have had all surviving airframes still in existence after retirement, either placed in storage or put proudly on display in a museum. Not one single airframe was ever scrapped.

NASA 844 taxis out for another mission. (NASA DFRC)

Chapter One

The Beginning

1 May 1960 proved to be more than just the traditional "May Day" in the Soviet Union. On that day, Russia proudly announced its confirmed capability for shooting down the world's highest-flying spyplane, America's super-secret Lockheed U-2.

Well before CIA U-2 pilot Francis Gary Powers became a household name that year, the agency had been seeking a high-speed, high-altitude replacement. Not to be upstaged, the U.S. Air Force was also studying a Lockheed proposal for a Mach 2.5 liquid-hydrogen-

fueled recon aircraft. In late-1957, the CIA chose Lockheed and Convair for follow-on proposal development, with Lockheed's Skunk Works evolving as the winning team under the direction of its legendary Chief Designer Kelly Johnson.

Lockheed concepts for a sleek, titanium twin-engined Mach 3 aircraft that could fly at 90,000 feet were initially referred to as Archangel 1, Archangel 2, etc.; a carry-over from the name "Angel" originally given to the U-2. These designations were shortened to A-1, A-2, and so on. It was the A-12 (the twelfth configuration study in the series) that emerged as the "frozen" design that went on to become the winning proposal in late 1959. In January 1960, the CIA authorized construction of 12 of these revolutionary new aircraft and the Project was given the seemingly stodgy codename of *Oxcart*.

Kelly Johnson's Skunk Works had been in existence in some form for over a decade before work began on the original hydrogen-powered designs that eventually evolved into the Blackbird family. Among the many great aircraft produced by the Skunk Works are the XP-80 and XP-80A Shooting Star, YF-94C Starfire, XF-90 Penetration Fighter, XFV-1 "Salmon" VTOL Interceptor, X-7 ramjet-powered research missile, XF-104 Starfighter, and U-2 Dragon Lady. (Lockheed Martin)

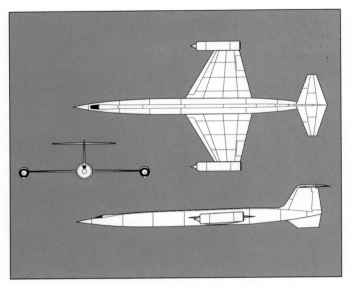

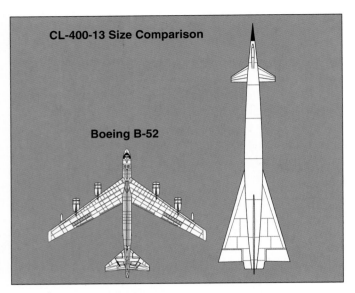

CL-400-13 Size Comparison

Boeing B-52

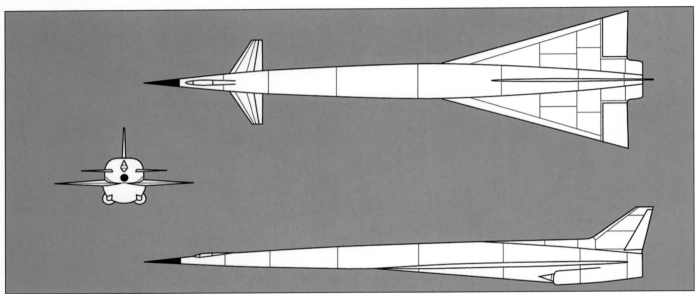

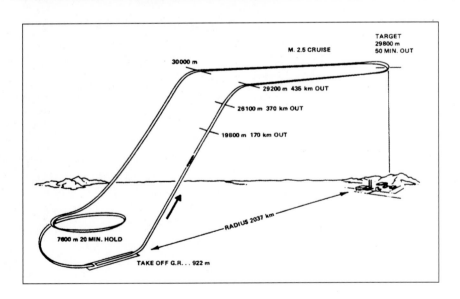

TARGET
29800 m
50 MIN. OUT

M. 2.5 CRUISE

30000 m

29200 m 435 km OUT

26100 m 370 km OUT

19800 m 170 km OUT

RADIUS 2037 km

7600 m 20 MIN. HOLD

TAKE OFF G.R. . . . 922 m

Project Suntan *called for the design of a high-speed, high-altitude aircraft, which was known internally as the CL-400. Numerous iterations of this design were investigated, including the CL-400-10 (top left) and the CL-400-13 (above). These designs were to be hydrogen powered and use the Pratt & Whitney Model 304 engine. None of these designs made it to the full-scale hardware stage, however. Left: This rough but rare diagram shows the proposed mission profile for Lockheed's CL-400 using liquid hydrogen as fuel.* (CIA Historical Archives)

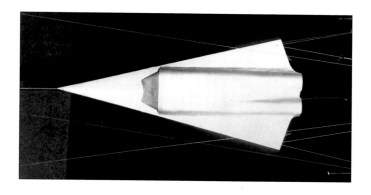

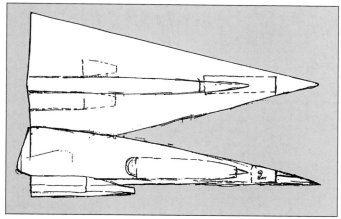

After the cancellation of Project Suntan, the engineers at Lockheed's Skunk Works got busy developing designs of a somewhat more conventional nature under Project Gusto. The "Arrow 1" design (above left and right) became the first of the new series followed by the Archangel 1 and Archangel 2 design configurations a short time later. Eventually, the nomenclature for these designs was simply shortened to A-1, A-2, and so on. Some concepts such as the A-7-3 (shown below in a crude but accurate technical drawing) differed only in small structural details, while others, such as the A-4 (shown in the very rough hand-drawn concept sketch at left), were completely new designs. As we will see, it took Lockheed until the twelfth design in this series to arrive at the final Blackbird configuration, hence the designation A-12 for the first Blackbird models built for the CIA. Note similarities to Lockheed's F-104 Starfighter in the wing and tailplane shapes. (Photos: Lockheed Martin; Artwork: Jay Miller Collection)

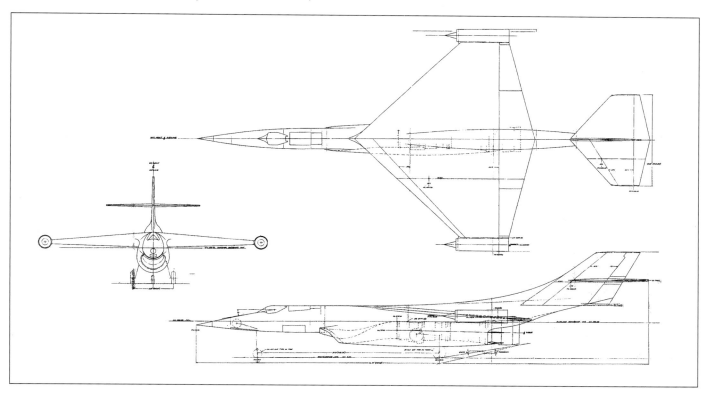

Lockheed's chief competitor on this project was General Dynamics with their early "Fish" design that would have been powered by two Marquardt ramjet engines and also carried two retractable J85 turbojets in the mid-fuselage giving it a maximum speed of Mach 4.0. This concept was to be air launched from a specially configured B-58 Hustler known as a B-58B. The Fish program was canceled due to impracticality of its size, propulsion system, and operational logistics. (Jay Miller Collection)

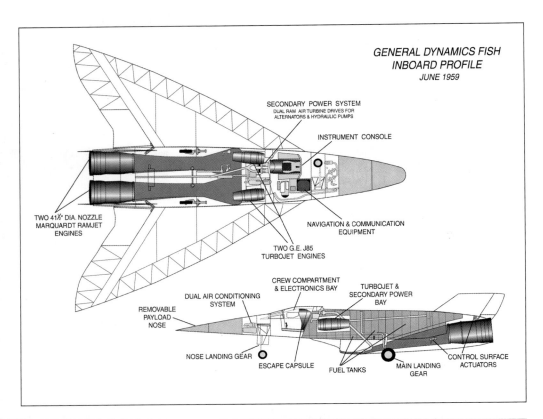

GENERAL DYNAMICS FISH
INBOARD PROFILE
JUNE 1959

SECONDARY POWER SYSTEM
DUAL RAM AIR TURBINE DRIVES FOR
ALTERNATORS & HYDRAULIC PUMPS

INSTRUMENT CONSOLE

TWO 41½" DIA. NOZZLE
MARQUARDT RAMJET
ENGINES

NAVIGATION & COMMUNICATION
EQUIPMENT

TWO G.E. J85
TURBOJET ENGINES

CREW COMPARTMENT
& ELECTRONICS BAY

DUAL AIR CONDITIONING
SYSTEM

TURBOJET &
SECONDARY POWER
BAY

REMOVABLE
PAYLOAD
NOSE

NOSE LANDING GEAR

ESCAPE CAPSULE

FUEL TANKS

MAIN LANDING
GEAR

CONTROL SURFACE
ACTUATORS

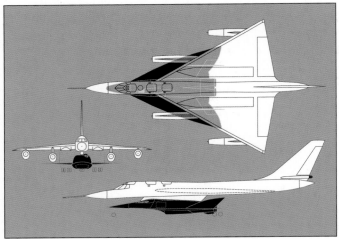

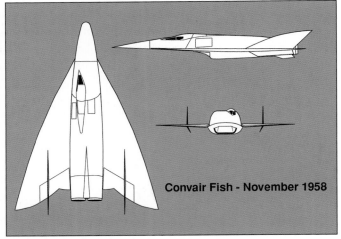

Convair Fish - November 1958

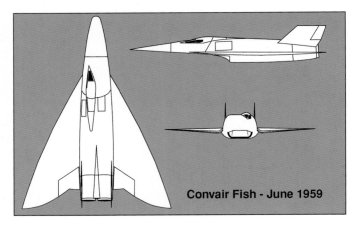

Convair Fish - June 1959

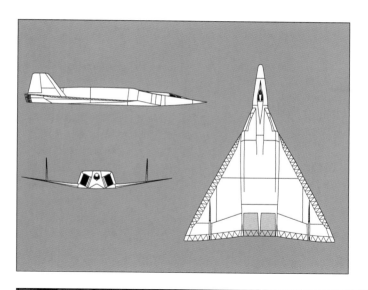

After the Fish concept was abandoned, a major redesign effort was undertaken by General Dynamics resulting in the J58-powered Kingfish. This aircraft did away with the ramjets as well as the need for a B-58 mothership and would have been capable of flight at Mach 3. This concept made it to the full-scale, pole-model stage before it too was canceled in favor of the Lockheed design. (Jay Miller Collection)

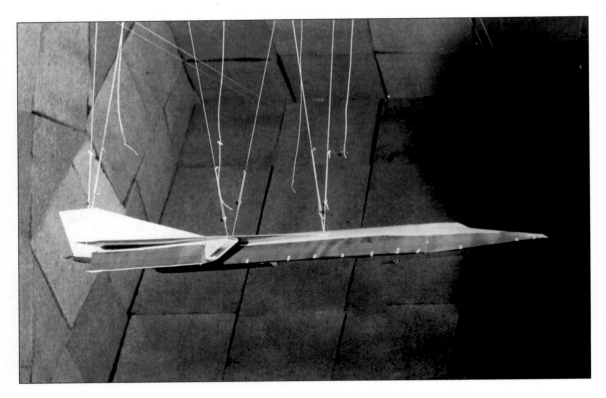

A modified A-10 design hangs inside the Lockheed anechoic chamber for early RCS testing. This design was tested with and without anti-radar coatings; this photo shows the model being tested with the coatings in place. (Lockheed Martin)

In this historical photo, an early development model of the ninth version of the A-6 configuration (right) sits next to an early A-12 model (left). The evolution of the design is very evident even at this early stage, with the full-body chine and twin vertical stabilizers. (Lockheed Martin)

A number of rough configuration models were built using the basic A-11 design. These were used by Lockheed engineers for testing various aerodynamic and radar cross-sections of the evolving aircraft. Many of these models were constructed as modular designs so that new airframe configurations could be tested without the need for constructing an entirely new model from scratch.
(Lockheed Martin)

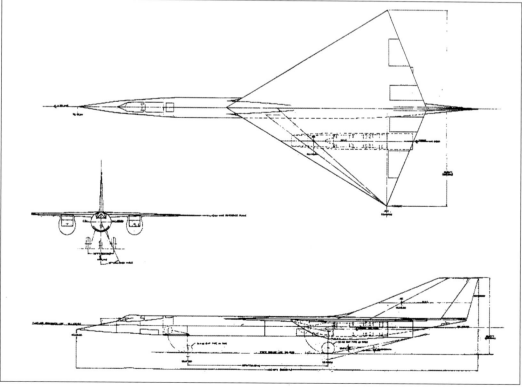

One of the numerous A-11 concepts was the A-11A shown here in a crude but accurate technical drawing with a smaller delta wing and tail. This aircraft was to use the same General Electric J93 turbojet that powered the triple-sonic North American XB-70 in place of the Pratt & Whitney J58. Like the J58 variants, however, this design would have been capable of cruising at speeds of Mach 3.2 and rarefied altitudes of 85,000 to 95,000 feet. (CIA Historical Archives)

Chapter Two

A-12 CYGNUS
The CIA's *Oxcart*

Since Lockheed aircraft types were traditionally named after famous celestial bodies, Lockheed crewmembers working on the top-secret program tentatively named the A-12 *Cygnus* (the swan), a constellation in the northern celestial hemisphere. The project itself had been officially named *Oxcart* by company officials, however.

Regardless of the name, the single-seat A-12 emerged as the most advanced high-performance reconnaissance aircraft ever flown, with a cruising speed of Mach 3.2 at operational altitudes in excess of 80,000 feet. Flown by CIA pilots in the mid 1960s, nothing could touch the performance of this radical, new, and highly secret aircraft.

The A-12 would prove to be the ultimate design of looks and performance but this did not come easily. Since no previous aircraft had been built for this type of performance, every aspect had to be developed from scratch. From the production of an all-titanium airframe to the use of fuels that would not explode when heated, the A-12 presented challenges to even the most experienced engineer. From the outset the radar cross section was a driving factor in the design. In this heavily retouched photo, two camouflaged A-12s appear to be flying in formation over a desert landscape. In reality, this is a photo of one of the RCS pole models pasted-up against a sky background in two different places. Neither aircraft is real. (CIA Historical Archives)

Full-scale A-12 nose section without the chine sits on a pole installed on the RCS test range at Groom Lake. (Lockheed Martin)

This early pole model shows the original swept-back vertical stabilizers, which had not yet been canted in, and used rudders for control rather than the all-moving stabilizers that would become standard on the production aircraft. (Lockheed Martin)

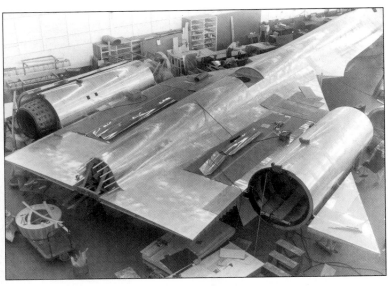

A primary area of concern for the CIA was the radar cross section (RCS) of the aircraft, and Lockheed spent many hours testing the design. Lockheed constructed a number of pole models for testing the RCS throughout the program, each becoming much more detailed as they progressed. Ultimately Lockheed placed an actual A-12 (Article 122, 60-6925) on the RCS pole to get detailed measurements from a production airframe (see page 22). (Lockheed)

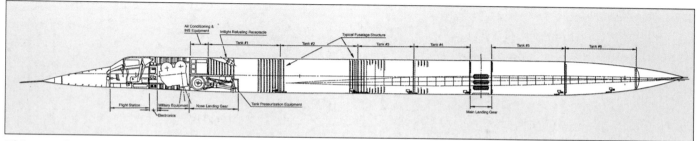

This rough inboard profile drawing of the A-12 reveals the layout of equipment installed inside the aircraft. In an age before miniaturization, the large and cumbersome camera apparatus was mounted directly behind the cockpit while the entire aft two-thirds of the fuselage was used primarily for storing fuel. Note triple-wheel main landing gear shown in the retracted position in the aft fuselage. (Jay Miller Collection)

As the design of the A-12 progressed, aerodynamic studies were performed on a number of wind-tunnel models. The top photo shows the final A-12 design while the photo above shows the A-12 model with a synthetic aperture radar (SAR) pod. (Lockheed Martin)

The first A-12 Article 121 (60-6924) is shown during the final assembly process at Lockheed's Skunk Works facility in Burbank, California. This was essentially a hand-built prototype as no hard tooling had yet been produced. (Lockheed Martin)

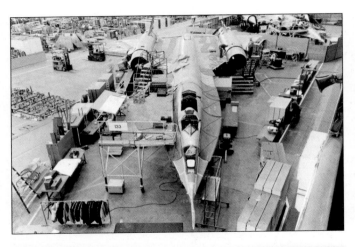

The A-12 assembly line at Burbank. At the time, this was the largest manufacturing program ever undertaken by the Skunk Works and it severely taxed their facilities. The chines on the A-12s were initially constructed with titanium wedge-shaped panels, but these were replaced by composite panels by the time the fifth aircraft was being assembled. Two of the first four aircraft, ships two and three, would later be retrofitted with the composite chine panels. (Lockheed Martin)

Article 121 under construction at Burbank. In order to install the titanium wedge-chine panels, Lockheed engineers developed a jig to ensure proper placement. Once completed, the A-12 would be partially disassembled for the trip to Groom Lake. (Lockheed Martin)

Because every part of the A-12 had to be developed from scratch, each item had to be tested to verify its design limitations. Here technicians set up the main landing gear assembly for another test. (Lockheed Martin)

Once each A-12 had been constructed and gone through a series of ground tests, the airframe was partially disassembled and placed inside specially built $100,000 transport containers for the trip to the Nevada test location. The trip from Burbank usually took about two days using public roads with the Highway Patrol for escort. (Lockheed Martin)

Initial engine runs and fuel system tests revealed a serious fuel leak problem that required the use of some external fuel tanks for ground testing. The aircraft was never flown with these installed. (Lockheed Martin)

Instrument panel of the first A-12 (Article 121, 60-6924) on 2 January 1962. Despite the advanced design, the cockpit used a relatively conventional layout. Because it was a single-seat aircraft the pilot had to fly the airplane as well as operate the camera system. (Lockheed Martin)

The first A-12 (Article 121, 60-6924) made its inaugural flight on 26 April 1962, with Lou Schalk at the controls, only getting to about 20 feet in altitude for about 1½ miles. The "official" first flight came four days later on 30 April. The aircraft was powered by two 17,000-pound-thrust Pratt & Whitney J75 engines since development problems had delayed the delivery of the larger and more powerful 20,500-pound-thrust J58s. During the early part of the flight test program, McDonnell F-101Bs were used as chase aircraft. (Lockheed Martin)

Early flight testing of the first A-12 progressed rapidly despite the use of the underpowered J75 engines. During the A-12's second flight on 4 May 1962, the jet achieved a speed of Mach 1.1 at 40,000 feet. The first in-flight refueling occurred during the twenty-fourth flight on 11 July. With the air refueling capability, missions could now be extended for hours. (Lockheed Martin/CIA Historical Archives)

The clean lines and all-titanium structure show up well in these views of the first A-12 (Article 121, 60-6924) taken on 10 July 1962. The bare-metal finish would only be used on the first four aircraft. Once the aircraft had been fitted with the composite chines, this area would be painted black. Eventually, all A-12s except for the two-seat trainer would be painted in an overall black scheme. The white spray emanating from the aircraft's tailcone (top) is fuel being dumped to allow the jet to land at its optimum landing weight. (Lockheed Martin)

The second A-12 (Article 122, 60-6925) was delivered to the test site on 26 June 1962. After a short flight program the aircraft was fitted with composite chines and leading edges and placed on the pole at the RCS range for several months of testing. (CIA Historical Archives)

Once the radar cross-section testing was completed in November, ship 2 joined the flight test program and was initially flown with two J75 engines. Note that the vertical stabilizers are made of composites as well. (Lockheed Martin)

The third A-12 (Article 123, 60-6926) arrived at the test site in late 1962 and like the previous two aircraft it was also flown with two J75 engines installed. This aircraft would be the first to be lost during a training flight on 24 May 1963, near Wendover, Utah, due to problems with the pitot static system. Pilot Ken Collins ejected safely. (Lockheed Martin)

The one-of-a-kind two-seat A-12 trainer to be constructed was Article 124 (60-6927). Nicknamed the Titanium Goose, it had a second crew station installed in the Q-bay, the pressurized area behind the cockpit, to allow its use as a trainer. The different finishes on this aircraft allowed optimum heat-sink capability as the Mach numbers increased. (Lockheed Martin)

The A-12 trainer Titanium Goose was the only A-12 not to be retrofitted with J58 engines, which limited it to Mach 1.6 and 40,000 feet. It was also only one of two not to receive the composite replacement panels since RCS was not a factor for this aircraft. (Lockheed Martin)

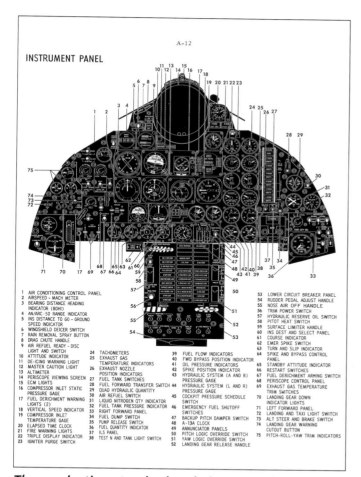

INSTRUMENT PANEL

A-12

1 AIR CONDITIONING CONTROL PANEL
2 AIRSPEED - MACH METER
3 BEARING DISTANCE HEADING INDICATOR (BDHI)
4 AN/ARC-50 RANGE INDICATOR
5 INS DISTANCE TO GO - GROUND SPEED INDICATOR
6 WINDSHIELD DEICER SWITCH
7 RAIN REMOVAL SPRAY BUTTON
8 DRAG CHUTE HANDLE
9 AIR REFUEL READY - DISC LIGHT AND SWITCH
10 ATTITUDE INDICATOR
11 DE-ICING WARNING LIGHT
12 MASTER CAUTION LIGHT
14 ALTIMETER
15 PERISCOPE VIEWING SCREEN
15 ECM LIGHTS
16 COMPRESSOR INLET STATIC PRESSURE GAGE
17 FUEL DERICHMENT WARNING LIGHTS (2)
18 VERTICAL SPEED INDICATOR
19 COMPRESSOR INLET TEMPERATURE GAGE
20 ELAPSED TIME CLOCK
21 FIRE WARNING LIGHTS
22 TRIPLE DISPLAY INDICATOR
23 IGNITER PURGE SWITCH
24 TACHOMETERS
25 EXHAUST GAS TEMPERATURE INDICATORS
26 EXHAUST NOZZLE POSITION INDICATORS
27 FUEL TANK SWITCHES
28 FUEL FORWARD TRANSFER SWITCH
29 QUAD HYDRAULIC QUANTITY
30 AIR REFUEL SWITCH
31 LIQUID NITROGEN QTY INDICATOR
32 FUEL TANK PRESSURE INDICATOR
33 RIGHT FORWARD PANEL
34 FUEL DUMP SWITCH
35 PUMP RELEASE SWITCH
36 FUEL QUANTITY INDICATOR
37 ILS PANEL
38 TEST N AND TANK LIGHT SWITCH
39 FUEL FLOW INDICATORS
40 FWD BYPASS POSITION INDICATOR
41 OIL PRESSURE INDICATORS
42 SPIKE POSITION INDICATOR
43 HYDRAULIC SYSTEM (A AND B) PRESSURE GAGE
44 HYDRAULIC SYSTEM (L AND R) PRESSURE GAGE
45 COCKPIT PRESSURE SCHEDULE SWITCH
46 EMERGENCY FUEL SHUTOFF SWITCHES
47 BACKUP PITCH DAMPER SWITCH
48 A-13A CLOCK
49 ANNUNCIATOR PANELS
50 PITCH LOGIC OVERRIDE SWITCH
51 YAW LOGIC OVERRIDE SWITCH
52 LANDING GEAR RELEASE HANDLE
53 LOWER CIRCUIT BREAKER PANEL
54 RUDDER PEDAL ADJUST HANDLE
55 NOSE AIR OFF HANDLE
56 TRIM POWER SWITCH
57 HYDRAULIC RESERVE OIL SWITCH
58 PITOT HEAT SWITCH
59 SURFACE LIMITER HANDLE
60 INS DEST AND SELECT PANEL
61 COURSE INDICATOR
62 EMER SPIKE SWITCH
63 TURN AND SLIP INDICATOR
64 SPIKE AND BYPASS CONTROL PANEL
65 STANDBY ATTITUDE INDICATOR
66 RESTART SWITCHES
67 FUEL DERICHMENT ARMING SWITCH
68 PERISCOPE CONTROL PANEL
69 EXHAUST GAS TEMPERATURE TRIM SWITCHES
70 LANDING GEAR DOWN INDICATOR LIGHTS
71 LEFT FORWARD PANEL
72 LANDING AND TAXI LIGHT SWITCH
73 ALT STEER AND BRAKE SWITCH
74 LANDING GEAR WARNING CUTOUT BUTTON
75 PITCH-ROLL-YAW TRIM INDICATORS

The production standard cockpit was well laid out with the instruments grouped accordingly. The large opening at the top of the panel was for the periscope viewing screen, which has yet to be installed here. (Photo: CIA Historical Archives; Artwork reproduced by Mick Roth)

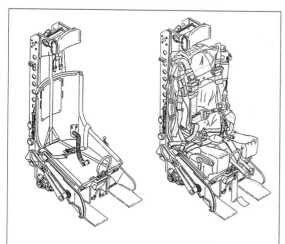

Tech art shows the A-12's modified, Lockheed-designed C-2 ejection seat, which evolved into the SR-1 seat used in the SR-71. Seat shell only is shown at left; seat with integral parachute, harness, and cushion at right. (Mike Relja Collection)

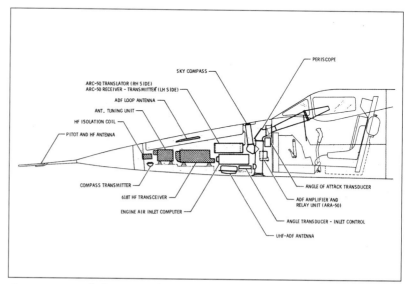

A cutaway of the A-12 forward fuselage showing the location of the communications equipment and periscope viewing system located in the nose of the aircraft. (Mike Relja Collection)

A-12 Article 125 (60-6928) taxis out for another mission at Groom Lake. This aircraft has been painted overall black, but only carries national insignia and tail number; it has yet to receive the U.S. Air Force stenciling on the fuselage. This aircraft and its pilot, Walter Ray, were lost on 5 January 1967, when a faulty fuel gauge caused the aircraft to run out of fuel on approach to landing. (Lockheed Martin)

An unidentified A-12 takes the runway at Groom, followed closely by its McDonnell F-101B chase aircraft. Note the absence of all markings except for rescue data applied near the cockpit and the small white article number applied to the tip of the nose. A second A-12 can be seen going through preflight checks in the background. (Lockheed Martin)

Perkin-Elmer Type I camera used two cameras imaging on a single stabilized platform and had a resolution of 1 foot at 80,000 feet. (CIA Historical Archives)

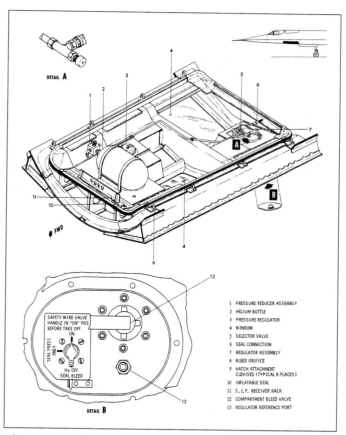

1	PRESSURE REDUCER ASSEMBLY
2	HELIUM BOTTLE
3	PRESSURE REGULATOR
4	WINDOW
5	SELECTOR VALVE
6	SEAL CONNECTION
7	REGULATOR ASSEMBLY
8	BLEED ORIFICE
9	HATCH ATTACHMENT CLEVISES (TYPICAL 8 PLACES)
10	INFLATABLE SEAL
11	S. I. P. RECEIVER RACK
12	COMPARTMENT BLEED VALVE
13	REGULATOR REFERENCE PORT

The camera bay cover for the Perkin-Elmer Type I consisted of a single camera window angled a few degrees to the left. (Mike Relja Collection)

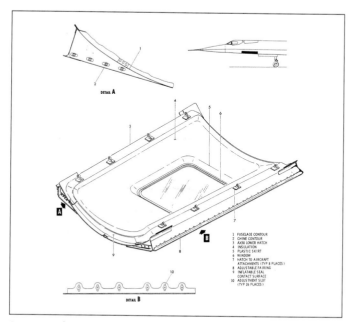

In case the Type I camera did not work, Eastman Kodak was asked to build the Type II camera for the A-12. This camera used a single window as well. (Mike Relja Collection)

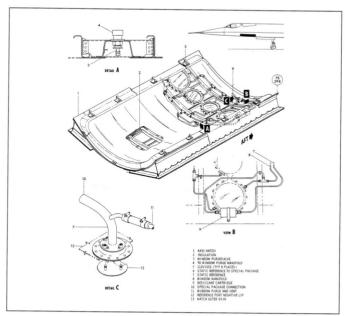

The Type III camera bay cover used multiple oblique and nadir camera windows. No documentation as to its actual use could be found. (Mike Relja Collection)

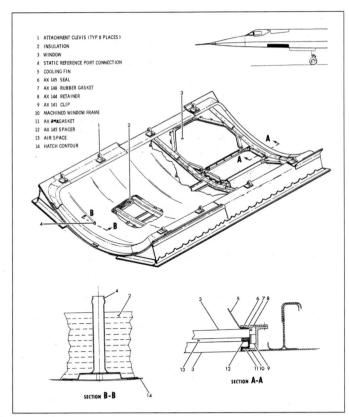

The camera bay cover for the Type IV camera built by Hycon used three windows providing wide coverage over the target area. (Mike Relja Collection)

Like the Type I camera, the Eastman Kodak Type II camera used two cameras imaging on a single platform and had a similar resolution capability. (CIA Historical Archives)

The A-12 and YF-12 aircraft lined up at Groom Lake in late 1963. Of particular interest is the fact that the aircraft are lined up in numerical order according to tail number. The closest aircraft is the first A-12 (60-6924) followed by the two-seat trainer Titanium Goose, then six more single-seat A-12s, and the first two YF-12As. The third YF-12A and last three A-12s have yet to join the fleet. The only other airframes missing are 60-6925, which had been used for RCS testing, and 60-6926, which had been lost earlier that year. (Lockheed Martin)

Two A-12s undergo routine maintenance work inside a hangar at the test site. The A-12 on the right is 60-6929, which was lost during takeoff on 28 December 1965. (CIA Historical Archives)

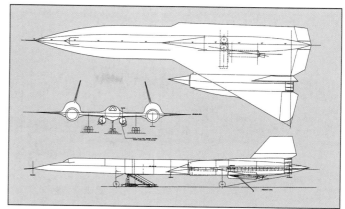

Lockheed's proposal to sell the A-12 to the U.S. Navy, known as the A-12CB (carrier based), shows the launch cradle position, tailhook, and JATO bottles beneath the fuselage. (Jay Miller Collection)

A-12 Article 129 (60-6932) holds formation behind the tanker. This aircraft was the last A-12 to be lost on 5 June 1968 when it disappeared during a functional check flight out of Kadena AB, Okinawa. CIA pilot Jack Weeks was killed. (Lockheed Martin)

The first two A-12s fly in formation over the Nevada desert with an F-104 chase plane. Barely visible is that ship 1 is still overall natural metal while ship 2 has the composite panels and is in the two-tone, natural-metal-and-black scheme. (CIA Historical Archives)

A-12 Article 130 (60-6933) is parked outside of the Oxcart hangers at Groom Lake. The distinctive natural-metal-and-black scheme was applied to all of the A-12s after the composite areas were installed on the aircraft. (Lockheed Martin)

After the A-12 program was terminated, all of the remaining airframes were flown to Lockheed's Palmdale, California, facility and placed in flyable storage. (Lockheed Martin)

The distinctive sharp-nose profile unique to the A-12 shows up well in this view of A-12 60-6932 as it pulls away from the tanker. (Lockheed)

After spending a few years sitting outdoors, the A-12 fleet was placed inside a large hangar at Palmdale. Note the fictional red serial number used on some operational aircraft. (Lockheed Martin)

The A-12 fleet spent more than a decade in flyable storage inside the hangar at Palmdale before Lockheed finally moved them all outdoors. Each aircraft was sealed in a protective coating to keep out moisture and the aircraft were parked around the facility. In some cases parts had been removed from the A-12s in order to support the SR-71 program. (Author)

All of the A-12s were eventually transported to various museums across the country. Article 122 (60-6925) was transported by barge to its new home aboard the aircraft carrier USS Intrepid *(CV-11) in New York harbor.* (USS *Intrepid* Collection)

Most of the surviving A-12s were disassembled by WorldWide Aircraft Recovery. They were moved to a vacant area of Air Force Plant 42 and had wings removed and engine nacelles cut off, then spliced back on once they arrived at their new home. (Mike Relja)

A-12 Article 128 (60-6931) was originally allocated to the Minnesota Air National Guard Museum and was disassembled by a crew of volunteers from that facility. With the wings and nacelles removed the fuselage was transported to the museum inside a Lockheed C-5 Galaxy. A second C-5 carried the wings and nacelles. In 2007, the aircraft was moved to CIA headquarters in Virginia. (Author)

At Palmdale in 1991 a lineup of two SR-71s and two A-12s await disassembly by a crew from WorldWide Aircraft Recovery. Each of the Blackbirds will be transported by truck to their new homes. (Mike Relja)

Because the A-12 fuselage would be too long for transport, the forward fuselage was removed and loaded aboard a flatbed in order to move it to its new location. (Mike Relja)

The only place in the world to see an A-12 and an SR-71 on display together is at the Blackbird Airpark in Palmdale, California. A-12 60-6924 (right) and SR-71A 61-7973 (left) are seen here on display. (Author)

Initially used as a source of spare parts for other museums, 60-6937 was restored by volunteers at Lockheed before being moved to the Southern Museum of Flight in Birmingham, Alabama. (David Allison)

A-12 60-6938 was allocated to the USS Alabama (BB-60) Battleship Memorial Park in Mobile, Alabama. In 2005, the A-12 was damaged by Hurricane Katrina but was restored by volunteers. (Owen Miller)

The sole two-seat A-12 trainer was one of the last A-12s to be moved to a museum. It spent many years in outside storage at Lockheed's Skunk Works facility in Palmdale before finally being moved to the California Science Center in Los Angeles, California. The raised second cockpit and all-titanium structure show up well in this view. (Kevin Helm)

One of the first A-12s to be put on public display was A-12 60-6933, which was placed outside of the San Diego Air & Space Museum in California. (Author)

In 2007, A-12 Article 128 (60-6931) was moved from the Minnesota Air National Guard Museum and displayed at CIA headquarters, Langley, Virginia. (CIA Museum)

Chapter Three

M-21 and D-21
Tagboard and Senior Bowl

In an attempt to augment and improve the A-12's mission yield, various studies were conducted by Lockheed to extend the range and operating envelope of the aircraft with an unmanned drone. This concept resulted from the need for an unmanned surveillance aircraft after the previously mentioned shootdown of a U-2 by the Soviet Union in May 1960, and resultant cancellation of manned reconnaissance flights over that country. One Lockheed study included the possibility of launching a modified pilotless QF-104 Starfighter from the back of the A-12, although the CIA expressed no interest in that idea whatsoever. What did emerge as the solution to this problem was a Mach 3 ramjet-powered drone

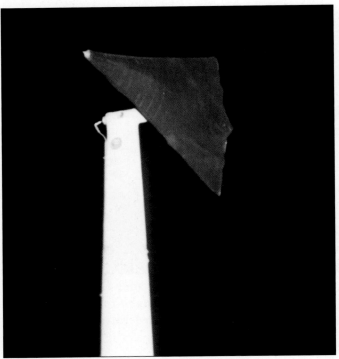

Like the A-12, the D-21 design began as a completely different layout than what was finally produced by the Skunk Works, and was more of a delta wing planform rather than the double-delta that evolved later. (Lockheed Martin)

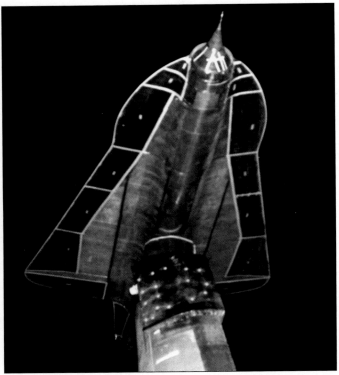

Lockheed built a full-scale RCS pole model of the production-configuration D-21 drone, which was tested on the RCS range at Groom Lake. (Lockheed Martin)

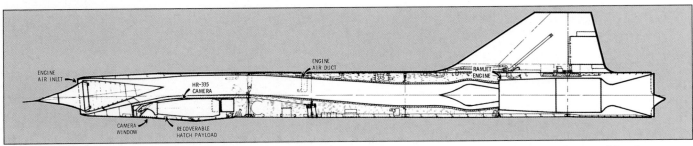

Inboard profile of the D-21 drone. Almost all of the electronic and camera systems were located in the recoverable hatch on the forward fuselage. The rest of the vehicle was primarily engine, inlet, and fuel. (Lockheed Martin)

developed specifically to overfly the Soviet Union and China. Known as the D-21, the new aircraft's aerodynamic lines closely resembled those of its A-12 launch aircraft.

Conceived to be launched at high speeds and altitudes from the A-12 mothership (redesignated as an M-21), D-21s were mounted to the upper rear fuselages of M-21s and released inflight. Initial tests yielded less-than-successful results. An alternative carrying-and-launch method was then devised, using underwing pylons mounted to inboard hardpoints on the wings of two Boeing B-52H Stratofortresses. Solid rocket boosters mounted below the D-21s were necessary to accelerate the drones to supersonic speeds where their ramjet engines would ignite and propel them on their way. Recovery methods for the reconnaissance packages jettisoned from the D-21s inflight are detailed in this chapter.

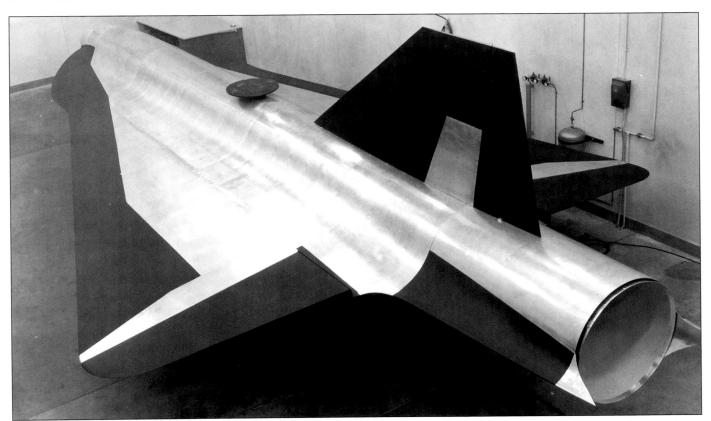

Full-scale wood-and-metal mockup of the D-21 drone known internally at the time as the Q-12. The mockup differed little from the actual aircraft with changes made to the inlet and vertical stabilizer, and removal of the circular antenna on the top of the fuselage. (Lockheed Martin)

The D-21s were constructed using structures that could be rotated 90 degrees to ease the assembly process. (Lockheed Martin)

For the first test fit, the inlet cone and composite leading edges were removed to prevent damage. (Lockheed Martin)

The first D-21 (501) is mated to the center pylon of the M-21 mothership for the first time. Initial ground checks were completed by engineers at the Skunk Works facility in Burbank prior to shipping the aircraft to the Nevada test location. (Lockheed Martin)

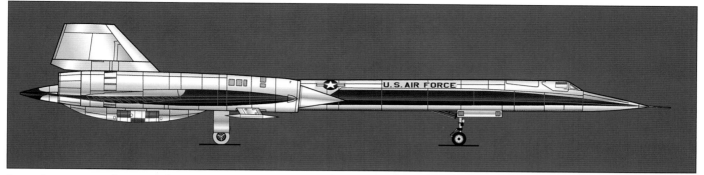

In order to test the parachute system for the recoverable hatch on the D-21, a single A-12 was modified with a ventral pod that could release the hatch at proper speed and altitude. A total of four drops were made with this system with all but the first being successful. Because no photos of this modification could be located, the above artwork was created based on interviews with program personnel. (Author)

The second D-21 (502) was used as the static test article. This D-21 went through structural tests at Lockheed's Skunk Works plant in Burbank. These tests used hydraulic jacks in various places to induce the loads that were to be encountered in flight. (Lockheed Martin)

The first D-21 (501) was simply wrapped and loaded onto a flatbed for transport to Groom Lake, unlike the A-12s, which had custom-built transport trailers. (Lockheed Martin)

Mounting a D-21 to an M-21 was tedious and time consuming. Only six inches of clearance existed between the drone's wingtips and the M-21's vertical stabilizer tips. (Lockheed)

Surrounded by Air Force B-1 and B-4 stands as well as aircraft ground equipment, the first M-21 (60-6940) is checked over by ground crews prior to the first flight with the D-21 (501) drone. When mated, the combination was referred to as the M/D-21 and the program was given the code name Tagboard. Although this aircraft was technically an A-12 when built, the added rear cockpit gave the appearance of a later SR-71. (Lockheed Martin)

Ground testing is completed on the M/D-21 at Groom Lake. Note that the bypass vents have all been masked over on both the M-21 and the D-21. (Lockheed Martin)

Initially, the D-21s were fitted with frangible fairings that would be pyrotechnically removed prior to launch. A failed attempt to remove them in flight curtailed their later use. (Lockheed Martin)

Red protective covers were used on the composite chines, wing leading edge, windscreen, intakes, and navigation window to prevent any damage to the aircraft during preflight and ground testing operations. (Lockheed Martin)

Numerous test missions took place with the mated pair to gather the necessary aerodynamic data prior to the actual test-launch missions. The first launch did not occur until 16 March 1966, more than 14 months after first flight. (Lockheed Martin)

Above: The M/D-21 lines up alongside its F-104 safety-chase aircraft prior to another winter test mission out of Groom Lake. F-104s replaced the F-101B Voodoo as safety-chase aircraft prior to the start of the M-21 flight program. (Lockheed Martin)

Left: The aft cockpit of the first M-21 (60-6940) after being restored by museum volunteers. (David Allison)

The M/D-21 during its first flight from the Nevada test site. This was performed late in the afternoon of 22 December 1964. The flight had been delayed by the first SR-71A flight, which took place at Palmdale earlier that same day. (Lockheed Martin)

Inflight refueling was an important part of each mission. The D-21 was a high-drag payload that adversely affected performance. (Lockheed Martin)

The first and last time an attempt was made to pyrotechnically remove the frangible nose cone resulted in heavy damage to the composite leading edges of D-21 503. (Lockheed Martin)

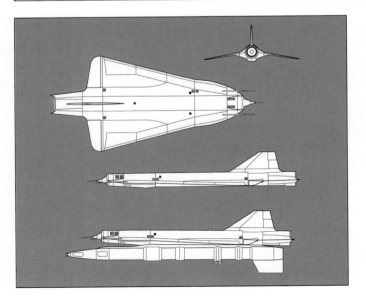

The second M-21 (60-6941) lines up on the runway at the Nevada test site. This aircraft was lost during a failed D-21 (504) test launch on 30 July 1966, thus ending the M/D-21 program. Film footage from various test launches show that this aircraft did carry the U.S. Air Force stenciling prior to its loss. Note over-wing camera pods housed inboard of the engine nacelles used to film the D-21 launches. (Lockheed Martin)

Three-view drawing of the D-21B. Lower artwork shows the D-21B with the solid rocket booster attached. (Author)

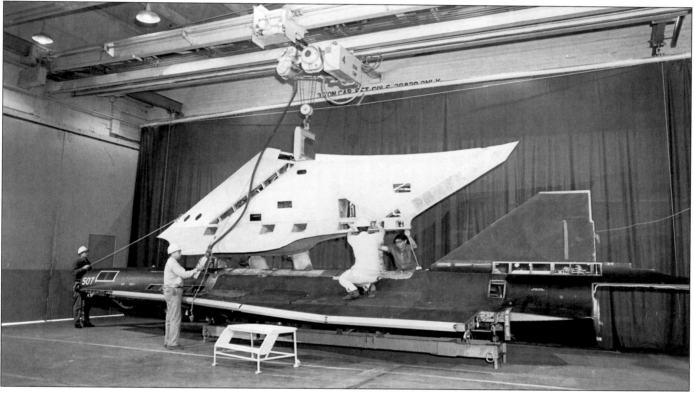

After the loss of the second M-21 in a mid-air collision with the D-21, the remaining airframes were converted for launch from a Boeing B-52H and designated D-21B. The new program was code named Senior Bowl. The D-21s were converted into B models in assembly-line fashion. Along with the drone conversion, Lockheed had to develop and construct the B-52H launch pylons as well as the solid rocket boosters needed to propel the drones to launch speed. (Lockheed Martin)

Without the high speed of the M-21 to get the D-21's ramjet engine up to speed, a solid rocket booster had to be developed for use with the D-21B. The solid rocket boosters were constructed by the Lockheed Propulsion Company in Redlands, California. The new booster was known internally as the Avanti and given the unofficial designation of A-92. Once assembled the new booster was placed in a vertical test stand and fired for the first time. (Lockheed Martin)

The new Avanti A-92 solid rocket booster is test-fitted to D-21B 501 for the first time at Lockheed's Skunk Works facility in Burbank. (Lockheed Martin)

Two Boeing B-52H Stratofortresses were allocated to the Senior Bowl program, 60-0036 and 61-0021. Modifications included the installations of two launch pylons, cameras to film the release, and D-21 operator stations. (Lockheed Martin)

The Launch Control Officer's station inside B-52H 61-0021. Cameras were installed in the pylons and in fuselage fairings to allow the LCO to monitor the launch. (Lockheed Martin)

A flurry of preflight activity surrounds B-52H 61-0021 prior to a D-21B mission from Groom Lake. Note the large air-conditioning unit being pulled into position in front of the B-52H. Keeping the systems in both the B-52H and the D-21s cool enough to operate properly was a big challenge during long, hot summer days in Nevada. (Lockheed Martin)

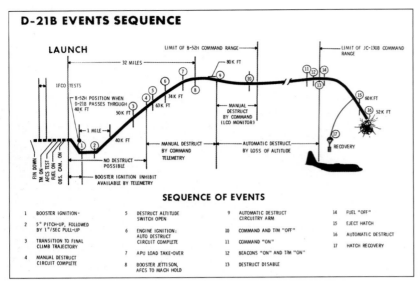

D-21B EVENTS SEQUENCE

LAUNCH

LIMIT OF B-52H COMMAND RANGE

LIMIT OF JC-130B COMMAND RANGE

32 MILES

80 K FT

IFCO TESTS

B-52H POSITION WHEN
D-21B PASSES THROUGH
40 K FT

74 K FT

63 K FT

50 K FT

60 K FT

52 K FT

1 MILE

MANUAL DESTRUCT
BY COMMAND
(LCO MONITOR)

40 K FT

RECOVERY

FIN DOWN
TM ON
AFCS TEST
FUEL ON
OBS. CAM. ON

NO DESTRUCT
POSSIBLE

MANUAL DESTRUCT
BY COMMAND
TELEMETRY

AUTOMATIC DESTRUCT
BY LOSS OF ALTITUDE

BOOSTER IGNITION INHIBIT
AVAILABLE BY TELEMETRY

SEQUENCE OF EVENTS

1. BOOSTER IGNITION
2. 5° PITCH-UP, FOLLOWED BY 1°/SEC PULL-UP
3. TRANSITION TO FINAL CLIMB TRAJECTORY
4. MANUAL DESTRUCT CIRCUIT COMPLETE
5. DESTRUCT ALTITUDE SWITCH OPEN
6. ENGINE IGNITION: AUTO DESTRUCT CIRCUIT COMPLETE
7. APU LOAD TAKE-OVER
8. BOOSTER JETTISON, AFCS TO MACH HOLD
9. AUTOMATIC DESTRUCT CIRCUITRY ARM
10. COMMAND AND T/M "OFF"
11. COMMAND "ON"
12. BEACONS "ON" AND T/M "ON"
13. DESTRUCT DISABLE
14. FUEL "OFF"
15. EJECT HATCH
16. AUTOMATIC DESTRUCT
17. HATCH RECOVERY

The recoverable hatch for the D-21B carried most of the flight control electronics, parachute recovery system, and Hycon HR-335 camera. (Jerry Miller)

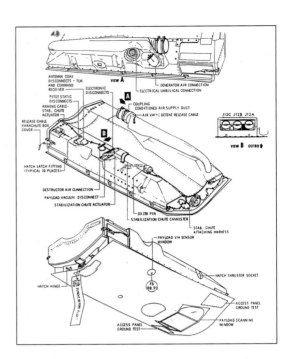

The Senior Bowl B-52Hs were capable of carrying and launching two D-21Bs on separate mission profiles. Visible on the bottom of each booster is the folded ventral stabilizer. (Lockheed Martin)

D-21B 501 hangs from the left pylon of a B-52H (61-0021) launch platform. This was the first D-21 built and the first converted into the B configuration; it has the Lockheed Propulsion Company Avanti A-92 booster attached. Unfortunately this D-21B and booster were accidentally dropped due to a stripped nut during a test flight on 28 September 1967. (Lockheed Martin)

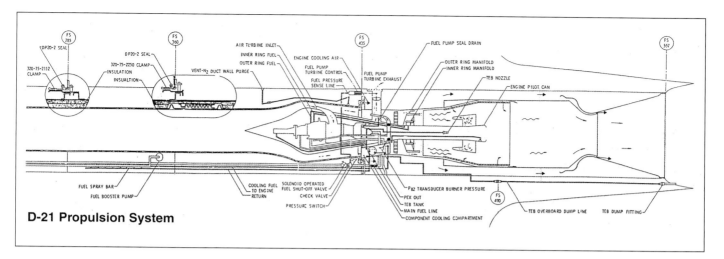

D-21 Propulsion System

A Senior Bowl B-52H carries two D-21Bs (515 and 518) over the ocean for a mission on 15 December 1968. During this flight D-21B 515 would be launched and fly nearly 3,000 miles before returning its payload to the drop point to be captured by an awaiting DC-130 and then flying to destruction into the Pacific. The returned imagery was considered to be of fair quality. (Lockheed Martin)

This view of D-21B 501 mated to Senior Bowl B-52H 61-0021, taken from the "boomer's" position of the KC-135 tanker, is reminiscent of the pylon assembly utilized for carrying and launching the North American X-15 research aircraft. (Lockheed Martin)

The Avanti A-92 solid rocket booster for the D-21B generated 27,300 pounds of thrust for 87 seconds, propelling the drone to a speed of Mach 3.2. (Lockheed Martin)

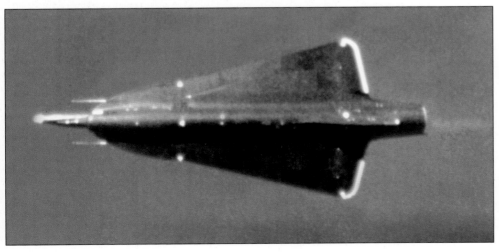

This view of a D-21B during launch was taken by a camera installed in the launch pylon of the B-52H. Solid rocket booster ignition took place two to four seconds after release. (Lockheed Martin)

After the final D-21B mission on 20 March 1971, the Senior Bowl program was terminated and the remaining D-21B drones were shipped to Norton AFB in California for storage. (Lockheed Martin)

In 1976, the Air Force decided to transfer the remaining drones to the storage center at Davis-Monthan AFB, Arizona. Prior to the transfer the Air Force had already prepared a briefing sheet that outlined what information could be disclosed about these vehicles, which came in quite handy when they were "accidentally" discovered by a group of aviation photographers several months later. (Mike Relja)

In June 1994, four D-21s (522, 525, 529, and 537) were delivered via C-17 transport to NASA's Dryden Flight Research Center for possible use as high-speed test vehicles. (NASA DFRC)

The D-21B was a relatively large aircraft, as shown in this view of a D-21 parked next to a Lockheed F-104G at NASA's Dryden Flight Research Center. (Author)

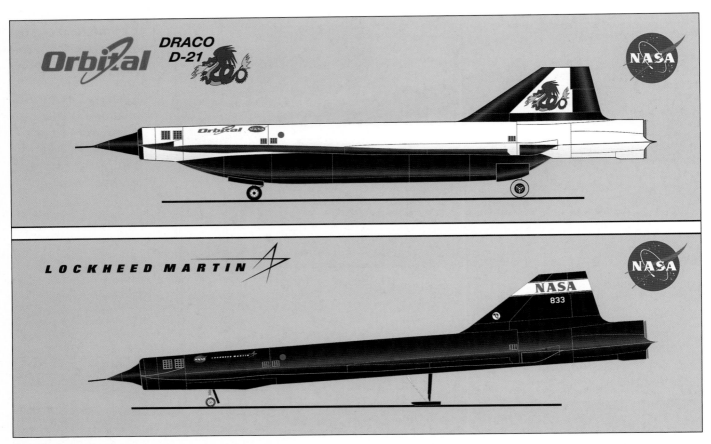

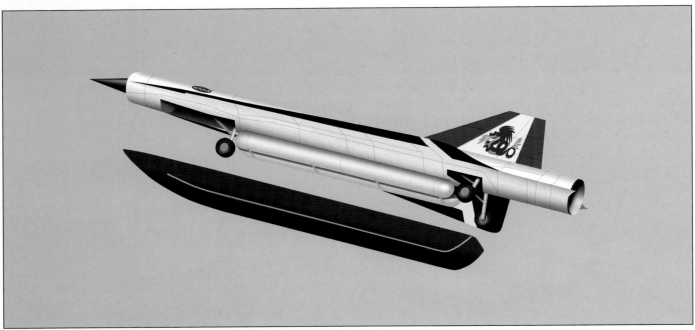

In 1999, NASA's Marshall Space Flight Center considered using a D-21 for testing a new RBCC (rocket-based combined cycle) engine that combined a ramjet and a rocket in the same flow path under the DRACO (Demonstration of Rocket and Air-breathing Combined-cycle Operation) program. Proposals were received from Orbital Sciences and Lockheed Martin for making the drone recoverable. The Orbital approach (bottom) used a fairing beneath the drone to cover extra fuel tanks and retractable landing gear, whereas Lockheed Martin went with a simple landing skid/nosewheel arrangement. (Top and Middle: Author; Bottom: Tom Tullis)

With no use for the D-21s, NASA returned them to the Air Force in 2006. Prior to their return, the USAF asked NASA to remove the Marquardt ramjet engines since their white inlet spikes contained a trace amount of mildly radioactive magnesium-thorium. The engines were shipped to Wright-Patterson AFB and subsequently scrapped. (Author)

In April 2007, two D-21s were kept for display and the other two drones were loaded onto trucks and shipped back to Davis-Monthan AFB for storage. (Author)

One remaining D-21B (525) was given to the Blackbird Airpark while the other (537) was sent to the museum at March ARB, California, for display. (Mike Relja)

Chapter Four

YF-12
Advanced Manned Interceptor

During the early 1960s, as the dynamics and tensions of the Cold War intensified, the need for an ultra-high-speed manned interceptor aircraft became paramount. Known as "The black sheep of the Blackbirds," the YF-12 was a weapon-carrying version of the A-12 that possessed the capability of climbing to altitude at Mach 3, locking-on to multiple targets at long range, and firing nuclear-tipped air-to-air missiles to vanquish the aerial foe, sight-unseen. Utilizing an advanced Hughes radar system originally designed for the stillborn North American XF-108 Rapier, Lockheed designed a new nose section to accommodate the large radar dish, giving the YF-12 a distinctly different appearance than that of its predecessor.

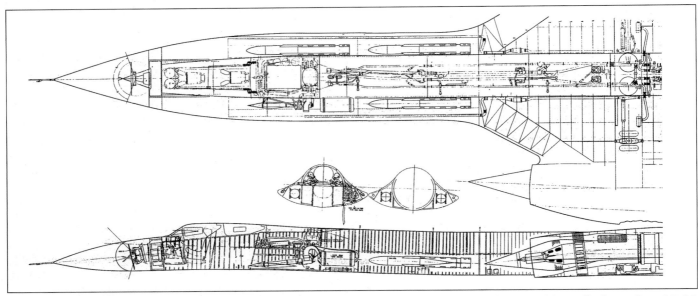

Rough but accurate engineering drawing from the AF-12 proposal shows the unusual installation of an M-61 20mm rotary cannon equipped with 1,000 rounds of ammunition in the forward-left weapons bay only. Three radar-guided Hughes AIM-47B air-to-air missiles are shown in the other three bays. (Lockheed Martin)

This Lockheed artist's concept of the AF-12 shows the early rounded chines. The area around the cockpit was painted black for anti-glare purposes. (Lockheed Martin)

The original nose mockup for the AF-12 used the same nose profile as the A-12 but has a missile hanging from a lowered launch rack in the aft fuselage. (Lockheed Martin)

The official veil of secrecy for the entire Blackbird Program was lifted in February 1964 when President Lyndon B. Johnson announced to the world the existence of the exotic new aircraft, but what appeared in those very first fuzzy and innocuous photos released to the public was, in actuality, the YF-12 interceptor flying in a bare-metal color scheme. Despite the unparalleled success of nearly all early YF-12 test missions, the Air Force canceled the program in January 1968, leaving the manned interceptor mission to the supersonic Convair F-106s of the Air Defense Command. The three YF-12s built were then used by NASA for high-speed and high-altitude flight test research.

The AN/ASG-18 fire-control system used in the YF-12A was originally developed for the stillborn North American Aviation F-108 Rapier Mach 3 interceptor, which never progressed beyond the full-scale mockup stage. (National Archives)

To test the Hughes AN/ASG-18 fire-control system, a single Convair B-58 Hustler (55-665) was modified by extending the nose to carry the radar and constructing two specially configured pods to house and launch the AIM-47 missile. The nose modification added nearly 7 feet to the bomber's overall length. (Left: Jim Eastham Collection; Above: Jay Miller Collection)

During the assembly of the YF-12s, the second airframe (60-6935) was curtained off from the rest of the production line for security purposes. Personnel involved in the YF-12A program were not cleared for the still-classified A-12. (Lockheed Martin)

The first YF-12A (60-6934) as it appeared prior to its maiden flight at the Nevada test site on 7 August 1963. Note the natural-metal fuselage and chines (instead of black) and the lack of any markings except the serial number on the vertical stabilizer. (CIA Historical Archives)

Lockheed test pilot Jim Eastham brings the first YF-12A (60-6934) in for a landing after its maiden flight at Groom Lake on 7 August 1963. Eastham was the second pilot to fly the A-12 and the primary test pilot for the AIM-47 tests using the modified B-58. (Lockheed Martin)

Lockheed built small models of the YF-12A, as they did with its predecessors, to be tested in the anechoic chamber. (Lockheed Martin)

This one-tenth-scale model of the YF-12A had special coatings applied prior to testing inside the anechoic chamber. (Lockheed)

Shortly after the first few flights were completed, the first YF-12A (60-6934) received the distinctive black-painted chines and U.S. Air Force markings, and began a very aggressive flight test program, which included aerial refueling tests. (Lockheed Martin)

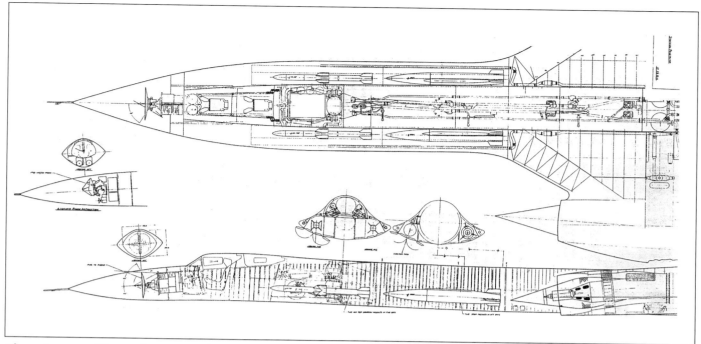

Plan view, profile, and cross sections of an early Blackbird bomber proposal called the FB-12-4 are shown in this rough but accurate Lockheed engineering drawing. Note the placement of the weapons and the original A-12 chine shape. The weapon arrangement has two AIM-7 E/F Sparrow missiles in the forward bays and AGM-69 SRAM missiles in the aft bays. (Lockheed Martin)

Shortly after being delivered to Edwards AFB in early 1964, the three YF-12As were painted black overall with U.S. Air Force markings. Sporting its new paint job, YF-12A (60-6934) is shown over the snowy Mojave Desert on 26 February 1965. (Lockheed Martin)

The second YF-12A (60-6935) on approach to Edwards AFB. The center ventral stabilizer is folded for landing, an automatic function when the landing gear is extended. (AFFTC History Office)

The Hughes AIM-47 missile was the predecessor of the AIM-54 Phoenix (left). The AIM-47 was 12.5 feet long, had a fin span of 33 inches, and weighed over 800 pounds. Its Mach 4 maximum speed was not significantly faster than the YF-12A that was launching it. The YF-12As launched seven of these in the course of the test program and six came within lethal distance to the target. (Lockheed Martin)

The second YF-12A (60-6935) parked on the ramp at Groom Lake. At this point, the markings were nearly identical to the ones carried by the A-12. (Lockheed Martin)

When President Johnson announced the existence of the "A-11," two of the YF-12s were hastily flown to Edwards AFB. Here the third YF-12A (60-6936) arrives at Edwards. (Lockheed Martin)

The YF-12s were displayed to the public and VIPs for the first time at Edwards AFB on 30 September 1964. While the first and third YF-12s participated in ground and aerial displays, the second aircraft was on display in a hangar with the nose cone removed to show off the 40-inch radar dish of the AN/ASG-18 fire-control system to select VIPs. (Lockheed Martin/AFFTC History Office)

YF-12As differed from their A-12 predecessors in having a large radome for the Hughes AN/ASG-18 fire-control system and the cut-back chine for the infra-red search-and-track seekers, which were later removed as shown here. (Lockheed Martin)

The early-style, silver pressure suits made by the David Clark Company were very similar in appearance to those used by the X-15 crews and early Mercury astronauts. (Lockheed Martin)

Prior to the world speed and altitude record attempts, the Air Force painted a white cross on the bottom of the first and third YF-12As to help cameras track the aircraft. (Lockheed Martin)

Early morning preflight activity on the first and third YF-12As, at Edwards AFB. (Lockheed Martin)

The third YF-12A (60-6936) taxis past the control tower at Edwards AFB after completing another test mission. (AFFTC History Office)

Like the CIA A-12s, the three YF-12As had a short rear fuselage tailcone that did not protrude past the trailing edge of the wing. The cut-off chines are clearly evident from this angle, although production F-12Bs would have used chines that extended to the nose. The worn paint on the bottom of each engine nacelle is also noteworthy. (Lockheed Martin)

The pilot's control panel of the YF-12A. Note vertical strip-type instruments used for speed and altitude information. YF-12s were the only Blackbirds to use this type of instrumentation. (Lockheed Martin)

The aft cockpit of the YF-12A contained all of the controls necessary to operate the radar and missile systems, as well as the large scope for the AN/ASG-18 radar and navigation system. (Lockheed Martin)

The third YF-12 (60-6936) with the gear up and the ventral down over Edwards AFB. Prior to the availability of the YF-12s for use in the speed and altitude record attempts, Lockheed had proposed using either A-12 Article 121 (60-6924) or Article 129 (60-6932) designated as XSR-71s for the attempt. (Lockheed Martin)

The first and third YF-12As had been chosen for the world speed and altitude record attempts. The camera pods located under the engine nacelles had been removed. (Lockheed Martin)

The first YF-12A (60-6934) on display at Edwards AFB in February 1965. Note that the aircraft now has the ADC logo on the left vertical stabilizer; the AFSC shield was on the right. (Lockheed Martin)

With the gear nearly retracted and ventral fin just beginning to lower, YF-12A 60-6936 takes off from Edwards AFB for a record flight attempt on 1 May 1965. (Lockheed Martin)

While the first and third YF-12As were being used to set new world speed and altitude records the second YF-12A (60-6935) was put on static display with the North American XB-70A on 1 May 1965. This was the only time the two aircraft were seen together. (Lockheed Martin)

After setting several new speed and altitude records, the third YF-12A (60-6936) was adorned with mission markings on both sides of the fuselage, which contained the information about each of the new records it set. (AFFTC History Office)

Lockheed family portrait on the ramp at Edwards AFB. Posing with the first YF-12A (60-6934) are, from front to back, F-104A Starfighter (56-0766), U-2D Dragon Lady (56-6954), T-33A Shooting Star (56-3675), the Fulton Recovery System testbed HC-130H Hercules (64-14855), and the fifth C-141A Starlifter (61-2779). (AFFTC History Office)

The second YF-12A (60-6935) during a test flight out of Edwards AFB on 11 December 1969. Note the Air Force Systems Command (AFSC) shield and outstanding unit ribbon carried on the vertical stabilizer. (AFFTC History Office)

The third YF-12A (60-6936) lands at Edwards AFB after a mission. All of the Blackbirds utilized the 40-foot-diameter drag chute system to reduce landing roll and aborted-takeoff rollout distance. (U.S. Air Force)

On this classic Dell comic book cover, the three YF-12As save the world from an alien invasion. (Author's Collection)

YF-12A 60-6935 with the ventral fin extended during a test mission from Edwards AFB. It was later determined that the vertical stabilizers and smaller ventral fins provided enough directional stability to offset the shortened nose-section chines. (AFFTC History Office)

The AIM-47 was the largest air-to-air missile developed in the United States at the time. (Marty Isham)

This image of the third YF-12A (60-6936) provides a good view of the unique placement of the rescue markings. (Lockheed Martin)

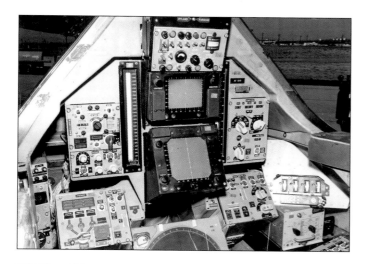

Official cancellation of the YF-12 program came in January 1968. Lockheed was instructed to stop all work on the F-12 and destroy all Blackbird tooling. NASA had been asking for use of two SR-71s for testing, but instead was allocated two YF-12s in a joint program with the US Air Force. All weapon system components were removed from YF-12A 60-6935 prior to the transfer. (Jerry McCulley Collection)

Once the YF-12s were ready for the joint NASA/Air Force test program, NASA pilots flew chase missions in their F-104s from December 1969 through February 1970 prior to taking over the flying duties. (NASA DFRC)

With John Manke flying chase in F-104N 812, YF-12A 60-6935 with Fitz Fulton and Ray Young in the cockpits, returns to Edwards AFB after another test mission. (NASA DFRC)

When two YF-12s were turned over to NASA, they wasted no time in putting their mark on the tail of YF-12A Ship 2. YF-12A Ship 3 was lost before receiving the same treatment. (NASA)

One of the first test programs undertaken by NASA upon receiving the YF-12s was the addition of a rear-facing camera on the lower fuselage adjacent to the nose landing gear. This camera measured the structural deflection of the fuselage during flight. (NASA DFRC)

YF-12A 60-6936 joined the joint test program on 3 March 1970. Of the 62 flights made by this YF-12A only six were made by NASA pilots before the aircraft was lost on 24 June 1971, due to a fire in the right engine. (NASA DFRC)

In 1996, the author was part of a small group that located the crash site of the third YF-12A. Surprisingly there were some rather large pieces left behind by the Air Force cleanup crews. (Author)

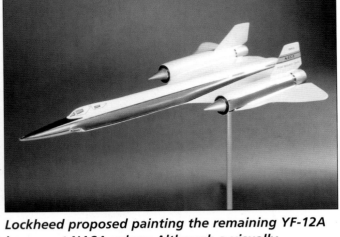

Lockheed proposed painting the remaining YF-12A in current NASA colors. Although a visually attractive scheme, one can only imagine the effect that routine maintenance and flight at speeds of Mach 3-plus would have had on that paint job. (Lockheed)

The surviving YF-12A was temporarily grounded after the loss of the third aircraft, so NASA used this time to perform a series of structural stress tests on the aircraft. The YF-12 returned to the flight program on 22 March 1971. (NASA DFRC)

Beginning with this mission on 7 April 1971, YF-12A 60-6935 began a short series of flights to test the stability of the aircraft without the large ventral fin installed. Handling qualities were found to be acceptable without the ventral fin, but it was reinstalled on the aircraft after only four test flights. (NASA DFRC)

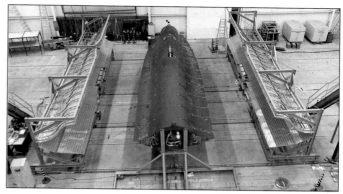

The largest ground test program undertaken by NASA to date was the structural heating tests done on YF-12A 60-6935. Lockheed and NASA constructed a custom-formed heating structure that conformed to the shape of the YF-12 fuselage. The forward fuselage of the first YF-12A (60-6934) was loaned to NASA for testing part of the heating structure. (NASA DFRC)

Lockheed constructed the aft portion of the heating structure at the Palmdale, California, facility and used SR-71A 61-7954 as the test article since it was no longer airworthy. (NASA DFRC)

Final assembly of the heating rig at NASA Dryden Flight Research Center comes together in December 1971. Note the forward fuselage of YF-12A 60-6934 inside the rig. (NASA DFRC)

By early 1971 the joint program with the Air Force had become mostly a NASA test program with Air Force crews only flying the aircraft one more time before it was returned to the USAF in 1979. (NASA DFRC)

YF-12A 60-6935 was grounded for more than a year—from February 1972 until July 1973—for the structural heating tests at NASA. Thousands of quartz lamps were used to heat the exterior structure of the aircraft as well as the insides of the engine nacelles. (NASA DFRC)

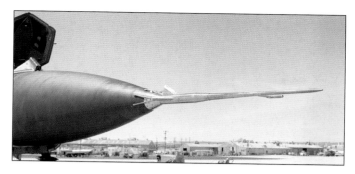

Test Probe

Once the YF-12A was back on flying status it proved to be quite versatile in adapting to the many and various test probes and experiments that NASA engineers placed onboard the aircraft. (NASA DFRC)

After the loss of the third YF-12A, NASA had requested a replacement aircraft. The second SR-71A (61-7951) was bailed to NASA but was given the fictitious designation of YF-12C and a bogus serial number, 06937, which had already been used by a CIA A-12. (NASA DFRC)

Graphic comparison of the YF-12A and SR-71A (known by NASA as the YF-12C). The most obvious differences from this angle are the cut-back chines and shorter aft fuselage of the YF-12A as well as the position of the refueling receptacle. (NASA DFRC)

One major flight test program for the YF-12A was a heat-transfer experiment known as Coldwall. Beginning in early 1975, NASA flew a stainless-steel tube instrumented with thermocouples and pressure sensors. During some tests the tube was covered in a special insulation and chilled to extremely cold temperatures using liquid nitrogen, which would be pyrotechnically removed at Mach 3.0. (NASA DFRC)

During a flight on 27 February 1975, YF-12A 60-6935 shed its ventral stabilizer but landed safely. The stabilizer was located and retrieved from the desert by NASA personnel and, after a series of flights to verify airflow around the aft fuselage, a new ventral stabilizer made of Lockalloy (a beryllium-aluminum composite material developed by Lockheed) was installed as a replacement. (NASA DFRC)

Late in 1976, YF-12A 60-6935 was modified with a water spray nozzle in the forward edge of the chine for vortex flow visualization studies. During this short test program YF-12C 06937 was flown alongside the YF-12A. (NASA DFRC)

The YF-12A and YF-12C were flown together on eight test missions between October 1976 and October 1977. During one flight on 21 July 1977 Coldwall insulation was ingested, which caused severe unstarts in both aircraft. Another test program that Lockheed proposed to NASA was a study of supersonic refueling using an adjustable boom on the YF-12C. These tests were never flown, however. (NASA DFRC)

YF-12C 06937 makes a final pass over NASA during its last NASA flight on 28 September 1978. (NASA DFRC)

Between June and September 1978, NASA engineers modified the YF-12A with the addition of small canards known as shaker vanes. These vanes were to help reduce the amount of turbulence absorbed by the airframe and, therefore, extend airframe life. (NASA DFRC)

Due to funding constraints, NASA canceled the YF-12A program in early 1979. The YF-12A was grounded from April to October 1979 while some instrumentation and the NASA tail art were removed. Prior to the final flight, NASA conducted a series of noise tests. (NASA DFRC)

The final NASA flight for the YF-12A was flown by Fitz Fulton and Vic Horton on 31 October 1979. (NASA DFRC)

On 7 November 1979, the sole surviving YF-12A was flown from Edwards AFB to the USAF Museum in Dayton, Ohio. (U.S. Air Force)

Chapter Five

SR-71 Blackbird
Mach 3 Masterpiece

Only eight months after the A-12's first flight in 1962, the U.S. Air Force ordered six "reconnaissance strike" versions of the new Blackbird for its own use. Code-named *Senior Crown*, this new aircraft would be slightly larger, heavier, and more capable than its predecessors. Additionally, it would be flown by a two-man crew with the RSO (Reconnaissance Systems Operator) in the back seat operating the aircraft's intelligence gathering equipment as well as its offensive and defensive countermeasures. One interesting distinction for the SR-71 was that it was the first of the Blackbirds to be tested at the new Air Force Plant 42 complex at Palmdale, California, rather than at Lockheed's remote desert test site.

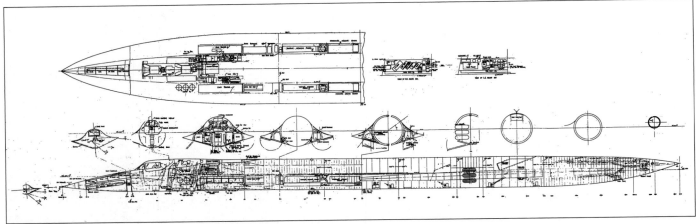

Plan view, profile, and fuselage cross sections showing the internal configurations of the SR-71A are depicted in this rough but accurate Lockheed engineering drawing. Larger and heavier than its predecessor, the SR-71 was a more versatile aircraft, carrying photographic, electronic intercept (Elint), and ECM equipment in multiple bays and interchangeable noses. (Lockheed Martin)

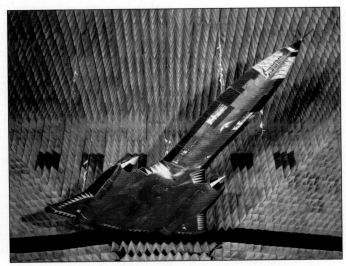

Many hours of testing were put into lowering the radar cross section of the SR-71. Scale models were placed in the anechoic chamber at Rye Canyon to test various components. (Lockheed Martin)

The full-scale engineering mockup of the SR-71A forward fuselage was used to test fit and check out all of the components that would be put into the actual aircraft. (Lockheed Martin)

Throughout the history of aviation, no other manned, jet-powered aircraft has ever flown higher or faster than the SR-71—the ultimate evolution of Lockheed's A-12. This final member of the Blackbird family firmly established itself as a benchmark in the design of manned air-breathing aircraft by setting world speed and altitude records in 1976 that will very possibly never be broken. As an operational aircraft having successfully flown more than 50,000 flight hours through hostile and denied airspace all over the world, the SR-71 ruled the skies for more than 35 years. It is highly conceivable that no other manned aircraft will ever take its place.

SR-71A wind-tunnel model being used to test the aerodynamics specific to this design. (Lockheed Martin)

All of the SR-71s were constructed in the same facility as the A-12 and YF-12. The forward fuselage was built separately from the rest of the airframe. Noteworthy are the protective panels placed over the chines to protect the composite skin during assembly. The open compartment just aft of the second cockpit is for the star-tracker navigation system. (Lockheed Martin)

Lockheed technicians prepare the first SR-71A (61-7950) to be painted prior to its first flight. (Lockheed Martin)

With the F-104 chase close behind, the SR-71A makes a low pass at Palmdale at the conclusion of its first flight. (Lockheed Martin)

First SR-71A (61-7950) during test flight out of Edwards AFB on 8 January 1965. Being the first test aircraft, it was relatively common to fly with the aft cockpit filled with test instrumentation. The small white stripe on the nose was unique to this SR-71A. (Lockheed Martin)

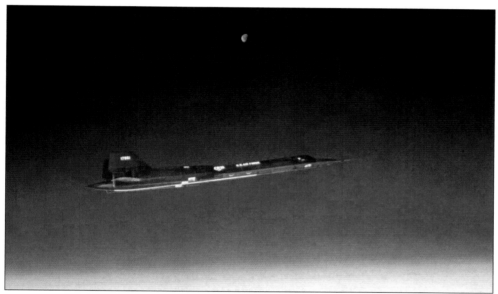

The primary aerodynamics test aircraft was the fully instrumented first SR-71A (61-7950) built. (Lockheed Martin)

The second SR-71A (61-7951) is shown during an early test mission prior to being bailed to NASA. (Lockheed Martin)

Upon its return from NASA, SR-71A 61-7951 made only one more flight before being placed in storage. (Lockheed Martin)

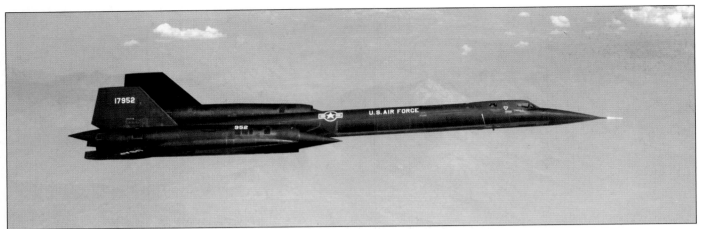

The third SR-71A (61-7952) was only with the flight test program for less than a year before it was lost on 25 January 1966 near Tucumcari, New Mexico. The aircraft was in a 60-degree bank at Mach 3.17 when it suffered an unstart, and the aircraft disintegrated. (Lockheed Martin)

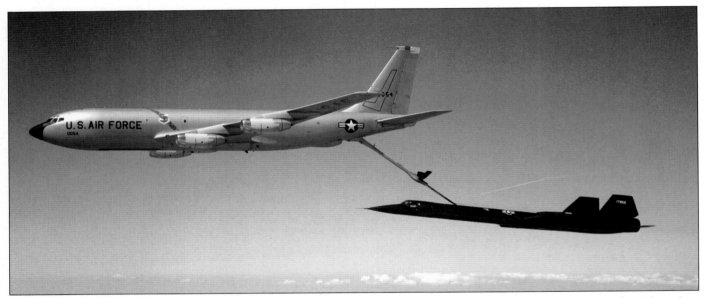

The first aerial refueling with an SR-71A was performed on 29 April 1965 using SR-71A 61-7952. (Lockheed Martin)

For tracking purposes the second, third, and fourth SR-71As had a white cross painted on the bottom. (Lockheed Martin)

SR-71A 61-7954 was one of the Air Force's two systems test aircraft and was first flown on 20 July 1965. (Lockheed Martin)

During a maximum weight takeoff test, the left main gear tires on 61-7954 blew, causing a fire that ultimately destroyed the aircraft. (U.S. Air Force)

The fourth SR-71A (61-7953) was the Air Force's equivalent of 61-7950 being instrumented for stability and control testing. This aircraft was lost on 18 December 1969 near Shosone, California. A civilian passing through the area at the time captured the accident on film. Air Force investigators were able to track him down since he had used a credit card to purchase gas at a local station. (U.S. Air Force via Bill Campbell)

SR-71A (61-7955) was the second systems test aircraft for the Air Force with full sensor accommodations. (AFFTC History Office)

A gloss-black U.S. Navy McDonnell F-4J Phantom II from famed test squadron VX-4 at Point Mugu, California, flies formation with SR-71A 61-7955 on 11 May 1972. (AFFTC History Office)

The fourth SR-71A (61-7955) was used as the primary flight test aircraft for its entire career, flying from Lockheed's Palmdale, California, facility. This aircraft was finally retired on 24 January 1985, after nearly 2,000 flight hours. (Bill Flanagan)

Two-ship formation with SR-71A 61-7955 and 61-7976 at the end of a test mission on 16 May 1975. (Lockheed Martin)

North American P-51 Mustang "Jeannie," one of the world's fastest piston-engine aircraft, flies with the world's fastest manned air-breathing aircraft. (Bill Flanagan)

Special markings were applied to SR-71B 61-7956 on the occasion of its 1,000th sortie on 15 January 1982. (U.S. Air Force)

The two SR-71B two-seat training aircraft undergo final assembly at Lockheed's Burbank facility (Lockheed Martin)

The first of two SR-71B two-seat training aircraft was initially flown on 18 November 1965, and delivered to Beale AFB, California, on 7 January 1966. When it was finally retired on 19 October 1997, it had amassed nearly 4,000 flight hours. (U.S. Air Force)

Part of every SR-71 pilot's training was to practice inflight refueling from the KC-135Q Stratotanker. (Bill Flanagan)

This cartoon pokes fun at SR-71 pilot B. C. Thomas as being chauffer to Aviation Week writer Robert Ropelewski. (BC Thomas Collection)

The second of two SR-71Bs (61-7957) during final assembly at Lockheed. First flight occurred on 10 December 1965. (Lockheed)

SR-71B (61-7957) lands at Beale AFB, California, after completing another pilot training mission. (Leland Haynes Collection)

Few photos exist of the second SR-71B (61-7957), since it was flown just two years before being lost in an accident on 11 January 1968. The aircraft suffered a double generator failure on approach to Beale AFB and the crew was forced to eject. (Lockheed Martin, left; Appeal/Democrat, right)

SR-71A 61-7958 was the first operational SR-71A delivered to the Air Force on 4 April 1966. (Lockheed Martin)

In July 1976, SR-71A 61-7958 was used to better three speed and altitude records previously set by the YF-12A. (Lockheed Martin)

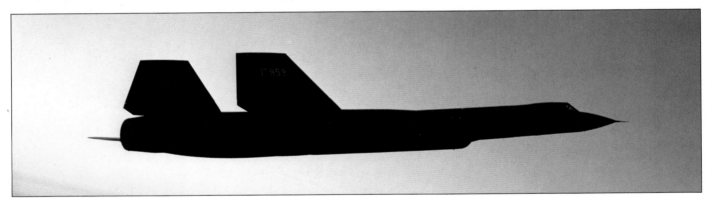

SR-71A 61-7959 was initially delivered to Beale AFB and flew for eight years before being transferred to flight test. (Lockheed Martin)

The "Big Tail" SR-71, 61-7959, sits at Palmdale minus its engines and outer wing panels after its final flight. The aircraft's vertical stabilizers were swapped with SR-71B 61-7956 at some point, and this airplane then apparently received an old tail fin from 956. (Lockheed Martin)

With the original tail section removed, Lockheed engineers added the new tail extension to SR-71A 61-7959. The new tail section was large enough to accommodate the 24-inch Optical Bar Camera along with aft-facing ECM equipment. The tail could be articulated 8.5 degrees upward or downward as required for takeoff or in-flight trim. The first flight took place on 5 May 1976, and the final flight was on 29 October. When it was retired it had the fewest flight hours of any surviving SR-71A, only 866.1 hours on the airframe. (Author)

The pilot's instrument panel of SR-71A 61-7967. The front cockpit was completely conventional in appearance, returning to round-dial instruments instead of the more exotic vertical tape instruments used in the YF-12A. (Author)

The SR-71B front cockpit was similar to the SR-71A but the aft cockpit (shown) differed slightly in appearance. (Author)

SR-71A 61-7960 spent a few months with flight test at Edwards AFB prior to being delivered to Beale AFB. (AFFTC History Office)

While departing Andrews AFB in 1984, 61-7960 suffered damage to the nacelle, which took weeks to repair. (Mike Relja Collection)

SR-71A 61-7961 flew operationally for nearly 11 years before being grounded and used as a source for spare parts in 1977. (Lockheed)

With the distinctive, white reference markings on the bottom, SR-71A 61-7962 departs Beale AFB. (Lockheed Martin)

SR-71A 61-7963 is prepared for another early-morning flight out of Beale AFB, California. (Lockheed Martin)

SR-71A 61-7964 on approach to RAF Mildenhall, which was the home of Detachment 4, 9th SRW. (U.S. Air Force)

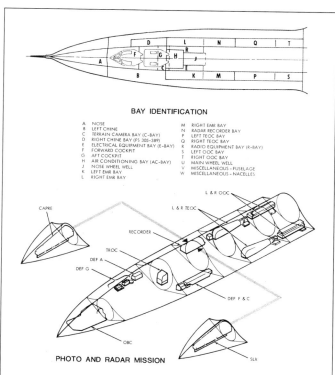

BAY IDENTIFICATION

A	NOSE	M	RIGHT EMR BAY
B	LEFT CHINE	N	RADAR RECORDER BAY
C	TERRAIN CAMERA BAY (C-BAY)	P	LEFT TEOC BAY
D	RIGHT CHINE BAY (FS 305-389)	Q	RIGHT TEOC BAY
E	ELECTRICAL EQUIPMENT BAY (E-BAY)	R	RADIO EQUIPMENT BAY (R-BAY)
F	FORWARD COCKPIT	S	LEFT OOC BAY
G	AFT COCKPIT	T	RIGHT OOC BAY
H	AIR CONDITIONING BAY (AC-BAY)	U	MAIN WHEEL WELL
J	NOSE WHEEL WELL	V	MISCELLANEOUS – FUSELAGE
K	LEFT EMR BAY	W	MISCELLANEOUS – NACELLES
L	RIGHT EMR BAY		

PHOTO AND RADAR MISSION

The SR-71A had a number of equipment bays for the variety of photographic and ECM equipment as well as its defensive electronics package. (U.S. Air Force)

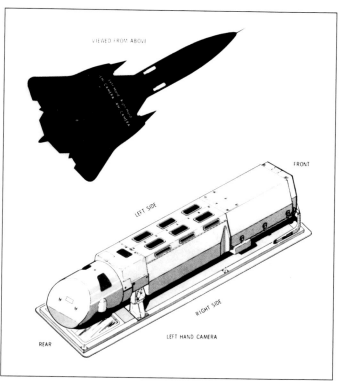

VIEWED FROM ABOVE

One of the primary photographic cameras carried by the SR-71 was the 48-inch-focal-length Technical Objective Camera (TEOC) carried in the forward chine bays. (U.S. Air Force)

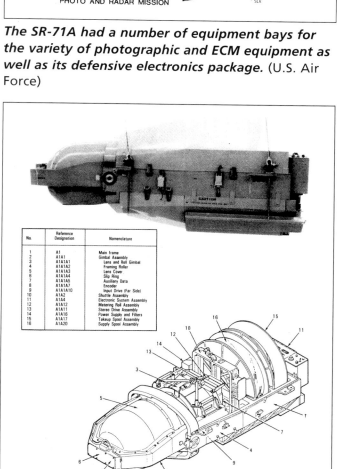

No.	Reference Designation	Nomenclature
1	A1	Main frame
2	A1A1	Gimbal Assembly
3	A1A1A1	Lens and Roll Gimbal
4	A1A1A2	Framing Roller
5	A1A1A3	Lens Cover
6	A1A1A4	Slip Ring
7	A1A1A5	Auxiliary Data
8	A1A1A7	Encoder
9	A1A1A10	Input Drive (Far Side)
10	A1A2	Shuttle Assembly
11	A1A4	Electronic System Assembly
12	A1A12	Metering Roll Assembly
13	A1A11	Stereo Drive Assembly
14	A1A16	Power Supply and Filters
15	A1A17	Takeup Spool Assembly
16	A1A20	Supply Spool Assembly

Optical Bar Camera

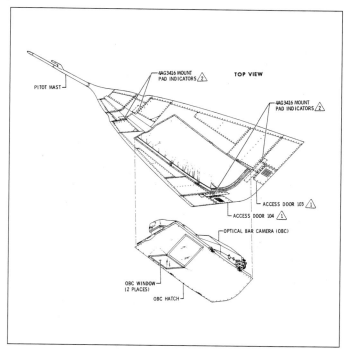

Mission planners could select from two different types of radar (CAPRE and ASARS) and two different Optical Bar Camera noses (left and above) to be flown on the SR-71A. (U.S. Air Force)

An SR-71A poses with some of the reconnaissance equipment carried on-board. Unlike the A-12s, which only carried photographic equipment, the SR-71 could carry a full range of photographic, radar, and signal intelligence gathering equipment. (Lockheed Martin)

Below: Two SR-71As (61-7967 and 61-7980) go through preflight operations prior to a mission from Kadena AB, Okinawa. (U.S. Air Force)

The reactivated SR-71s had the option of using a real-time data downlink system. The antenna cover was known as the Wart. (U.S. Air Force)

Left: SR-71A 61-7967 rendezvous with the awaiting KC-135 tanker prior to taking on a full load of JP-7. (Bill Flanagan)

SR-71A 61-7967 was temporarily assigned flight test duties to evaluate changes defined by the test program. (U.S. Air Force)

After being retired in 1990, 61-7967 was sent to Palmdale for storage and was frequently brought out for PR assignments. (Author)

Sporting the new low-visibility markings, SR-71A 61-7968 takes the runway at Kadena AB on 10 September 1986. (U.S. Air Force)

SR-71A 61-7969 taxis out for another mission. This aircraft was lost near Thailand on 10 May 1970. (Author's Collection)

SR-71A 61-7968 takes on fuel from a freshly painted KC-135Q somewhere over Northern California. (Lockheed Martin)

In-depth maintenance as well as modification and upgrade work for the SR-71 fleet was performed at Lockheed's Site 2 facility located on Air Force Plant 42 in Palmdale, California. Work was often performed next to the U-2R Dragon Lady maintenance. (Lockheed Martin)

With all of its protective covers and "Remove Before Flight" tags in place, SR-71A 61-7971 sits on the ramp at Beale AFB. This aircraft was turned over to NASA in 1990. (Doug Nelson)

The Pratt & Whitney J58/JT11D-20 engine for the SR-71 could generate up to 32,500 pounds of thrust in full afterburner. (Pratt & Whitney)

The distinctive green flash of TEB (triethylborane) needed to ignite the JP-7 fuel used by the SR-71's J58 engines. (Author)

Shock diamonds in the exhaust were clearly visible when running a Pratt & Whitney J58 at full afterburner. The aft section of the J58 engine would glow red hot and could reach temperatures near 3,200 degrees F. (Author)

Access to the SR-71's Pratt & Whitney J58 was facilitated by raising the entire outboard wing, which rotated upward almost 90 degrees from the horizontal position. (Author)

Engine runs of the J58 were an impressive sight made even more so when a small amount of JP-7 fuel was purposely ignited. (Author)

SR-71A 61-7972 taxis out for a mission at Kadena AB, Okinawa. This aircraft was one of two SR-71s to carry the small Habu mission markings (inset) on the left side of the forward fuselage. (U.S. Air Force)

On 1 September 1974, SR-71A 61-7972 made a non-stop flight from Beale AFB to RAE Farnborough, in which the New York-to-London segment was flown in 1 hour, 55 minutes. (Lockheed Martin)

When the decision was made to retire the flight test SR-71A (61-7955), the next SR-71A to require periodic depot maintenance (PDM) would become the test aircraft. SR-71A (61-7972) was flown to Palmdale in late 1984 and began flight test duties in January 1985. (Bill Flanagan)

SR-71A 61-7972 lands at the Norton AFB Open House. During a show in 1986, the SR-71 made a pass over the Thunderbirds so low and loud that it caused a few members of the team to hit the deck. In retaliation for this embarrassment the T-birds refused to begin until all of the SR-71's ground equipment was stored out of their view and placed inside the hangar in the background. (Left: Author; Right: Mike Relja)

SR-71A 61-7973 undergoes preflight checks prior to a mission out of Kadena AB, Okinawa. (U.S. Air Force)

The first SR-71 to receive the low-vis markings was 61-7973. The subdued insignia and "USAF" lettering were short-lived additions. (Lockheed)

During a portion of its operational career, SR-71A 61-7974 carried "Habu" mission markings and tail art showing "Ichi Ban," which means "number one," or "the very best" in Japanese. (U.S. Air Force)

In January 1984, SR-71A 61-7974 was flown to Ramstein AB, Germany, for a retirement ceremony. (Scott R. Wilson)

On 21 April 1989, SR-71A 61-7974 was on a routine flight off the coast of Southeast Asia when the left engine seized. The crew attempted to divert to Clark AB in the Philippines but were forced to eject as conditions worsened. The aircraft went down off the coast of Luzon in shallow water so the Air Force chose to retrieve the wreckage. A Navy salvage team retrieved the remains and brought it back to Kadena AB for examination. Ironically, once the accident investigation was completed, the wreckage was hauled back out into the Pacific and disposed of. (U.S. Air Force via Al Cirino)

Most of the operational Blackbirds spent time flying out of forward operating locations like Kadena AB on Okinawa and RAF Mildenhall in the United Kingdom. SR-71A 61-7975 was no different and was even caught (right) by the cameras of a high-flying McDonnell RF-4C while on the taxiway at Kadena. (U.S. Air Force)

On 21 March 1968, SR-71A 61-7976 was the first Blackbird to fly an operational mission over Vietnam. (U.S. Air Force)

Landing mishaps were pretty uncommon for the SR-71 and most were repairable like this event involving 61-7976. (U.S. Air Force)

Several SR-71s sported some tail art during their careers, including SR-71A 61-7976 with a stylized cat motif. (Lockheed Martin)

The end of the line. The last three SR-71As going through final assembly at Lockheed's facility in Burbank. (Lockheed Martin)

SR-71A 61-7977 was written off after suffering a wheel explosion and aborted take-off at Beale AFB on 10 October 1968. (U.S. Air Force)

The cockpit section of 61-7977 was salvaged from the wreck and stored in the Site 2 boneyard at Palmdale. (Author)

Nicknamed Rapid Rabbit for the Playboy bunny that was carried on its tail, SR-71A 61-7978 flew operational missions for the U.S. Air Force for over 15 years prior to being lost at Kadena AB, Okinawa, while attempting to land in severe crosswinds. (Lockheed Martin)

An attempt to dispose of the titanium and composite wreckage of SR-71A 61-7978 by fire was not very successful. (S. Pargetter)

SR-71A 61-7979, carrying the 9th SRW shield on its tail, departs Beale AFB, California, on 2 August 1981. (U.S. Air Force)

SR-71A 61-7980, carrying some very exotic tail art, taxis in after landing at Palmdale on 18 September 1969. (Lockheed Martin)

The last of its breed, SR-71A 61-7980 was the final SR-71 to come off of the assembly line at Lockheed. (Lockheed Martin)

Inflight portrait of the unique SR-71C 61-7981, which replaced the second SR-71B. (Lockheed Martin)

The one-of-a-kind SR-71C 61-7981, nicknamed The Bastard, was constructed to replace the second SR-71B, which had been lost in an accident. The aircraft used the aft fuselage from the first YF-12A (60-6934) and the forward fuselage mockup for the SR-71. (Lockheed Martin)

The SR-71 Blackbird program was officially terminated on 22 November 1989, nearly 22 years after the first operational sortie. A retirement ceremony was held at Beale AFB on 26 January 1990. For the first time in history nearly every surviving airframe was brought out of their individual hangers for a photographic session the following day. A failed attempt was made to have all of the airframes scrapped; instead, most of the Blackbirds were dispersed to museums across the United States. (Lockheed Martin)

The morning of the SR-71 group photo session brought a dense fog to Beale AFB, which threatened to cancel the entire event. As the first two SR-71As were put into position, the conditions on the flightline made for this very dramatic image. (Lockheed Martin)

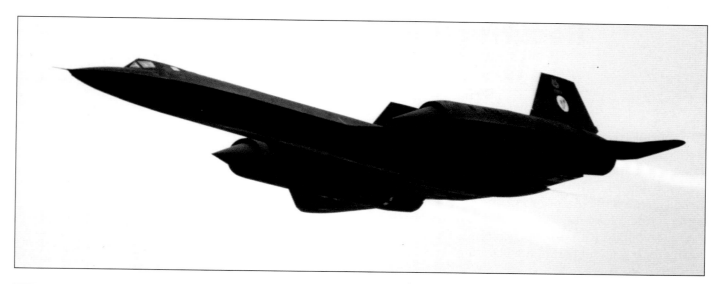

On 6 March 1990, SR-71A 61-7972 set new speed records on its retirement flight to the Smithsonian National Air and Space Museum in Washington, D.C. After departing Palmdale, California, the aircraft headed east and made the coast-to-coast run in 1 hour, 8 minutes for an average ground speed of 2,112 mph. After a low pass at Dulles Airport, the SR-71 was greeted by a large crowd of VIPs and spectators including the former chief of the Skunk Works, Ben Rich. (Top and Bottom Right: Author; Middle and Bottom Left: U.S. Air Force)

Chapter Six

Resurrection and Retirement
NASA and Det.2/9RW

In the final years of the Blackbird's existence, both the U.S. Air Force and the National Aeronautics and Space Administration made use of the world's fastest and highest-flying jet. With the advent of modern satellite surveillance and intelligence gathering in the late 1980s, however, the role of the SR-71 had become diminished. That fact, coupled with the rising costs and relative complexity for overall support of the Blackbird's mission, led to the aircraft's retirement by the Air Force in November 1989. In the decade that followed, a brief attempt was made to resurrect the Air Force mission, and three SR-71s were also loaned to NASA for advanced flight test research purposes.

For NASA, the airplane provided a high-speed research capability unlike any other vehicle in its inventory. The SR-71s also allowed the testing of new

After the Air Force terminated the Blackbird program, NASA acquired two SR-71As, 61-7971 and 61-7980, and the sole-surviving two-seat trainer SR-71B 61-7956 for research. The first SR-71A to arrive was 61-7980 on 15 February 1990, followed by 61-7971 a month later on 19 March 1990. It would be another year before the SR-71B was delivered to NASA. (Jim Ross/NASA DFRC)

When the SR-71 program was canceled, the SR-71B had been in Palmdale undergoing periodic depot maintenance. The Air Force covered the cost of reassembling the aircraft and making it flyable again. (Jim Ross/NASA DFRC)

propulsion technologies with devices that could be mounted atop the Blackbirds and flown at speeds of up to Mach 3. Numerous other valuable test programs were flown, including high-altitude experiments and sonic boom propagation studies. With the final flights of both USAF and NASA SR-71s in the late 1990s, the proud era of Lockheed's magnificent Blackbird family finally came to an end.

The first functional check flight out of Palmdale for the SR-71B took place on 1 July 1991, with Air Force Lt. Col. Rod Dyckman and NASA research pilot Steve Ishmael at the controls. For these check flights the aircraft had all of its U.S. Air Force markings removed and had not yet been given NASA markings. (Marta Bohn-Meyer/NASA DFRC)

SR-71B 61-7956 received a fresh coat of paint and new NASA markings prior to being delivered to NASA's Dryden Flight Research Center located on Edwards AFB. (Jim Bean/NASA DFRC)

Along with its new paint job, the SR-71B also received the NASA tail number of 831. Unlike the two SR-71As, this aircraft retained its original USAF number in small red numbers. (Jim Bean/NASA DFRC)

Sporting a new coat of paint and NASA markings, the SR-71B departs Palmdale on its delivery flight to NASA on 25 July 1991. (Author)

The drag chute package for the SR-71 consists of three separate chutes: a spring-loaded 48-inch pilot chute that deployed a 10-foot-diameter extraction chute, which in turn deployed the 40-foot-diameter ribbon-type main drag chute. (Marta Bohn-Meyer/NASA DFRC)

With the delivery of the two-seat trainer SR-71B complete, the two NASA pilots assigned to fly the aircraft, Steve Ishmael and Rogers Smith, can complete their check-outs and begin pilot proficiency training prior to beginning actual research missions. (NASA/DFRC)

Shortly after SR-71A 61-7971 was delivered to NASA, it was given some interim tail markings. These were just for display until the actual tail art could be applied and were never actually flown on the aircraft. (Author)

One of the first experiments flown on the SR-71A was a NASA JPL upward-looking ultraviolet video camera mounted in a modified nose compartment. (Carla Thomas/NASA DFRC)

The first NASA research flight for SR-71A 61-7980 (now NASA 844) was on 24 September 1992, and carried the laser air data collection system in a modified nose. The 1 hour, 40 minute flight reached a maximum speed of Mach 3.25. (Jim Ross/NASA DFRC)

The NASA Blackbird fleet posed together on the ramp at NASA's Dryden Flight Research Center in California. Only two of the three aircraft were flown for NASA, SR-71B 61-7956 (NASA 831) and SR-71A 61-7980 (NASA 844). (Carla Thomas/NASA DFRC)

The four NASA crewmembers initially assigned to the program—Steve Ishmael and Rogers Smith (pilots) as well as the research system operators (RSOs) Bob Meyer and Marta Bohn-Meyer—flew the SR-71B for proficiency and checkout. (NASA DFRC)

The SR-71 was an awesome sight to behold from any angle, but from head-on it looks 20 years ahead of its time, even today. The heat waves generated by the two Pratt & Whitney J58 engines are quite visible as NASA 844 taxis out for another mission. (NASA DFRC)

When NASA acquired their Blackbirds, they also took delivery of the only flight simulator and all of the associated computer systems to go with it. (Dennis Taylor/NASA DFRC)

SR-71A NASA 844 lands after a sonic boom test mission on 12 April 1995. Note the window in the modified nose for Dynamic Auroral Viewing Experiment (DAVE). (NASA DFRC)

During the first half of 1995, SR-71A NASA 844 was involved in a series of flights to determine the intensity of its sonic boom in flight. The SR-71A was flown with a General Dynamics F-16XL and a Lockheed YO-3A at lower altitudes. (Jim Ross/NASA DFRC)

The three aircraft used in the NASA sonic boom intensity studies—SR-71A, F-16XL, and YO-3A—are parked together on the ramp at Dryden Flight Research Center. (NASA DFRC)

Nearly all NASA flights of the SR-71 were accompanied by an F/A-18 chase aircraft. The F/A-18 could only stay with the Blackbirds during the early part of their missions. (Jim Ross/NASA DFRC)

In September 1994, more than four years after the Blackbirds were retired, Congress authorized the reactivation of three SR-71s and allocated $100 million dollars to that effort. Of the three SR-71s stored in Palmdale and the sole SR-71A NASA was not using (61-7971/NASA 832), the reactivation crews determined that 61-7971 and 61-7967 were in the best shape and would be the first two to be brought back into service. NASA crews ferried -971 back to Palmdale on 12 January 1995. After three month's work it was refurbished and back in the air, while -967 followed about seven months later. NASA aircrews performed the initial check flight as the Air Force crews were being requalified in SR-71B 61-7956, the use of which NASA now shared with the Air Force. (NASA DFRC)

SR-71A 61-7967 was the first aircraft delivered to the newly activated Detachment 2/9th RW at Edwards AFB. (Author)

Both of the reactivated SR-71As began flying operational test missions shortly after arriving at their new unit at Edwards AFB. (Author)

Despite the fact that the SR-71 reactivation efforts had come in ahead of schedule and under budget, Air Force officials made it very clear that they had no desire to use the aircraft operationally, and never added it to any operational mission plans. (Blair Bozek)

NASA and Air Force flight crews shared the use of the sole SR-71B two-seat trainer, which included some night qualification flights for the Air Force crews to be declared mission ready. (Left: Tony Landis/NASA DFRC; Right: Bob Meyer/NASA DFRC)

Unfortunately the Air Force reactivation efforts proved to be short-lived. The final blow came on 15 October 1997 when President Bill Clinton eliminated all funding with a line-item veto. The last USAF flight took place on 10 October 1997 in SR-71A 61-7967. All attempts to secure additional funding failed and the program held a final salute on 3 December 1998. (Author)

With a full moon over the Blackbird, its days as an operational Air Force asset were over. Detachment 2/9th RW was officially shut down on 30 June 1999. (Author)

The two reactivated SR-71As were once again parked on the ramp for storage. While they were flying, they had been given a BB tail code and Air Force standard serial numbers. (Author)

Making what would be its last appearance at the Oshkosh airshow on 2 August 1997, the SR-71B (61-7956) was flown behind a KC-135 during a simulated refueling pass. As the Blackbird began its climb out for the return trip to Edwards AFB, a fuel line ruptured, spewing raw fuel out of the left engine exhaust (top right). The aircraft made an emergency landing at Milwaukee Airport. A crew from NASA was then dispatched to repair the SR-71, which was flown back to Edwards AFB on 11 August. Showing a good sense of humor, upon egressing the SR-71 the aircrew donned their "Cheeseheads." (Jim Ross/NASA DFRC)

When Lockheed Martin won the contract to build the Linear Aerospike-powered X-33 reusable launch vehicle demonstrator, they wanted to test the engine in flight on the back of the NASA SR-71A. The original design had the engine placed close to the center of gravity but it was moved aft for safety reasons. (NASA DFRC)

Harking back to the heyday of the famed X-Planes at Edwards AFB in the 1950s, the LASRE was sent to the rocket test site at Edwards for ground testing prior to being test-flown on the SR-71. (NASA DFRC)

The first flight of SR-71A NASA 844 with the LASRE attached occurred on 31 October 1997. (Lori Losey/NASA DFRC)

On 25 May 1995, SR-71A NASA 844 was flown to Palmdale to be modified to carry the Linear Aerospike SR-71 Experiment (LASRE). The 10-month modification strengthened the aft fuselage and added mounting points to the fuselage. At this time the NASA tail art was changed as well. (NASA DFRC)

Considering the complexity of the LASRE modification, the aft cockpit received very few changes. (NASA DFRC)

NASA 844 departs Edwards AFB on 4 March 1998 for the first inert-gas "cold flow" test of the LASRE. Landings were made without the use of a drag chute due to the LASRE "canoe" covering the parachute doors. (NASA)

Inert gasses (nitrogen in the oxygen system plus helium instead of hydrogen) were used to test all of the plumbing inside of the LASRE pod before any hot fire could be attempted. (Carla Thomas/DFRC)

Closeups of the forward and aft mounting points on SR-71A NASA 844 for the Linear Aerospike Experiment. (Author)

Testing the Linear Aerospike engine proved to be as troublesome as the construction of the actual X-33 vehicle. Despite attempts to fix the problems as they arose, many proved to be insurmountable. With funding running out, the decision was made to cancel the LASRE program in November 1999. Cancellation of the entire X-33 demonstrator program followed 13 months later. The Aerospike engine was then returned to Lockheed and the aeroshell was stored. The "canoe" was also stored for a number of years before it was finally cut up and scrapped. (Jim Ross/NASA DFRC)

After the cancellation of the LASRE program, NASA engineers proposed using the "canoe" as an experiment platform. Five flights were made using the "canoe," only flying to Mach 3.03 at 67,800 feet. (Left: Carla Thomas/NASA DFRC; Right: Lori Losey/NASA DFRC)

The unplanned final flight for the SR-71 came on 9 October 1999 at the Edwards AFB open house. An attempt to fly the following day was canceled due to a severe fuel leak. NASA had plans to store the aircraft until new customers could be found, but none were ever located. On that final flight the aircraft flew to Mach 3.21 and 80,100 feet. (Left and above: Jim Ross/NASA DFRC; Right: NASA DFRC)

NASA had put their Blackbirds in flyable storage for a short time, which included occasional engine runs and systems checks. When it appeared that there would be no future use for them they were simply parked on the ramp for display. (Author)

Because of the unique ground equipment required to support SR-71 operations, NASA stored both their Blackbirds as well as the former USAF SR-71s. Eventually ownership was transferred back to the Air Force for all but one and they were allocated to museums. (Author)

A good comparison of the final tail art applied to the NASA and Air Force Blackbirds at the end of the program. NASA retained ownership of 61-7980 for display at Dryden. (Author)

In early 2003, the sole remaining SR-71B (61-7956/ NASA 831) was moved to Edwards AFB to be disassembled by WorldWide Aircraft Recovery for transport to the Kalamazoo Aviation History Museum in Michigan. (Left and Above: Author)

NASA placed the remaining SR-71A (61-7980/NASA 844) on static display in front of Dryden Flight Research Center in September 2002. On display with the Blackbird are two AG-330 start carts and a Pratt & Whitney J58 engine. (Left: Carla Thomas/NASA DFRC; Above: Author)

When NASA took delivery of their Blackbirds, they also inherited all of the spare parts. These parts were originally stored at Norton AFB until the base was closed in 1994 and the parts were moved to the Marine Corps Logistics Base in Barstow, California. Eight years after the Blackbird program ended, the Air Force accepted the responsibility of disposing of the two warehouses full of SR-71 parts. (Above Left, Above Right, and Left: Author)

Flying off into a beautiful California sunset is SR-71B 61-7956/NASA 831 during a night qualification flight on 16 November 1995. For more than 35 years the Blackbird family owned the skies. To this day it remains the fastest and highest-flying operational manned aircraft ever built. (Bob Meyer/NASA DFRC)

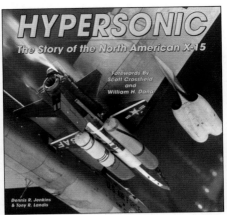
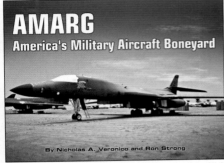
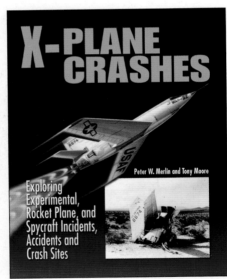
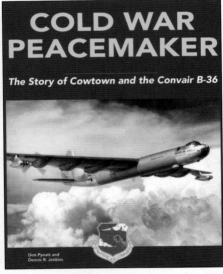
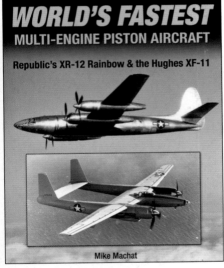